PRAISE FOR *BEYOND THE TREES*

"*Beyond the Trees* is a remarkable tale—and a staggering feat . . . It's mesmerizing to be guided through Canada's wilderness through Shoalts' eyes . . . Shoalts also wields a wicked wit." *ATLANTIC BOOKS TODAY*

"[*Beyond the Trees*] might just soothe your need for adventure . . . wonder-filled . . . [a] beautiful book." *BUZZFEED*

"A wild adventure . . . riveting." *MONTREAL GAZETTE*

"Adam Shoalts does what most of us would never dare to do . . . *Beyond the Trees* is a very readable homage to the wilds of the Canadian North." *RICHMOND NEWS*

"[A] rousing adventure story . . ." *CANADA.COM*

"Adam has a magic way of writing and making you feel like you are hiking through the wilderness with him." *BOOKS WITH COOKE*

" . . . the adventure of a lifetime [told] in thrilling detail." *TVO*

"[Shoalts] brings us along on his solo journey across the Arctic, infused with the wonder of seeing this majestic land and the urgency of making it back before winter sets in." *TORONTO STAR*

"His journey took him . . . across the terrestrial world's largest expanse of wilderness outside Antarctica . . . [an] engaging, hazard-strewn account." *NATURE*

"If you love an outdoor adventure, *Beyond the Trees* is for you." *KAMLOOPS MATTERS*

PRAISE FOR *A HISTORY OF CANADA IN TEN MAPS*

"It's an epic journey ... Shoalts has done an elegant job of ... reminding us of the vast and brooding influence of geography on our history." *THE GLOBE AND MAIL*

"Shoalts analyzes early maps in order to paint a picture of the land that would become a nation, bringing its earliest stories, voices, and battles to life. Combining geography, cartography, history, and anthropology, Shoalts leaves no stone unturned." *CBC*

"A brilliant book." *CANADIAN GEOGRAPHIC*

"[A] marvel ... If you like maps, you'll like this book; if you like both maps and crisply recounted Canadian history, you'll love it. Shoalts ... takes you inside [explorers'] heads as they face fear, doubt and despair in tandem with cold, starvation, and rebellious wanting-to-turn-back companions ... Canadian history writ well." *WINNIPEG FREE PRESS*

"A masterful approach to mapping Canada." *TORONTO STAR*

"[O]ne fine book perfectly written for the armchair adventurer." *POSTMEDIA*

"Adam Shoalts's book is a must read for anybody with interests in Canadian history, geography, and exploration." *CANADIAN GIS*

PRAISE FOR *ALONE AGAINST THE NORTH*

"Rare insight into the heart and mind of an explorer, and the insatiable hunger for the unknown that both inspires and drives one to the edge. Adam Shoalts . . . calmly describes the things he has endured that would drive most people to despair, or even madness." *COL. CHRIS HADFIELD*, astronaut, International Space Station commander

"As gripping to read as it must've been exciting to live!" *LES STROUD,* Survivorman

"Adam Shoalts's remarkable solo foray . . . is the kind of incredible effort that fosters legends." *WINNIPEG FREE PRESS*

"Shoalts's love of nature, cool professionalism, and almost archaically romantic spirit draw us into his adventures . . . Shoalts is a knowledgeable and observant guide." *QUILL & QUIRE*

"Anyone who thinks exploration is dead should read this book." *JOHN GEIGER*, author, CEO of the Royal Canadian Geographical Society

"The more layers you peel away, the more you begin to see the quick mind and quiet intensity that helps propel Adam Shoalts." *BRIAN BANKS, CANADIAN GEOGRAPHIC*

"It is a story of brutal perseverance and stamina, which few adventurers could equal." *LIFE IN QUEBEC MAGAZINE*

"Shoalts is a fearless adventurer . . . *Alone Against the North* is a rip-roaring yarn." *THE GREAT CANADIAN BUCKET LIST*

"Shoalts . . . vividly describes an area of the country most of us will never witness." *METRO* (Toronto)

PRAISE FOR ADAM SHOALTS

"One of Canada's greatest modern explorers." *CBC*

"Adam Shoalts is Canada's Indiana Jones—portaging in the north, dodging scary rapids, plunging into darkness, and surviving to tell the tale." *TORONTO STAR*

"Adam Shoalts is one heck of a paddler." *POSTMEDIA*

"Explorer Adam Shoalts's monumental 4,000-kilometre journey ... calls to mind the likes of Vilhjalmur Stefansson and Joseph Tyrrell." *CANADIAN GEOGRAPHIC*

"Move over Jacques Cartier, Christopher Columbus, and Sir Francis Drake—Adam Shoalts is this century's explorer." *HAMILTON SPECTATOR*

"Adam Shoalts ... [has] finished an incredible journey through Canada's Arctic." *GLOBAL NEWS*

"Shoalts is a skilled woodsman and naturalist, able to survive the northern wilds with rudimentary equipment." *CANOE AND KAYAK MAGAZINE*

ALSO BY ADAM SHOALTS

Beyond the Trees
A History of Canada in Ten Maps
Alone Against the North

THE
WHISPER
ON THE
NIGHT WIND

THE TRUE HISTORY OF A WILDERNESS LEGEND

ADAM SHOALTS

PENGUIN

an imprint of Penguin Canada,
a division of Penguin Random House Canada Limited

Published in this edition, 2022

Originally published in hardcover by Viking Canada, an imprint of
Penguin Random House Canada, Toronto, 2021. Distributed
by Penguin Random House Canada Limited, Toronto.

1 2 3 4 5 6 7 8 9 10

www.penguinrandomhouse.ca

Permissions for extracts granted from:
Hollett, L., eds. "Stories of the Mealy Mountains Akamiuapishkᵁ."
Them Days, Stories of Early Labrador 30 no. 2 (2006).

Rompkey, R. *The Labrador Memoir of Dr Harry Paddon*, 1912-1938.
Montreal: MQUP, 2003. Print.

All interior images are courtesy of Adam Shoalts unless otherwise stated.

LIBRARY AND ARCHIVES CANADA CATALOGUING IN PUBLICATION

Title: The whisper on the night wind : the true history of a
wilderness legend / Adam Shoalts. Names: Shoalts, Adam, 1986- author.
Description: Previously published: Toronto: Allen Lane Canada, 2021.
Identifiers: Canadiana 20210092068 | ISBN 9780735241060 (softcover)
Subjects: LCSH: Shoalts, Adam, 1986-—Travel—Newfoundland and Labrador.
| LCSH: Legends—Newfoundland and Labrador. | LCSH: Newfoundland and
Labrador—Description and travel. | LCSH: Newfoundland and Labrador—History.
Classification: LCC FC2167.6 .S56 2022 | DDC 917.18/2047—dc23

Book design by Emma Dolan
Cover image © stsmhn / iStock / Getty Images Plus

Printed in the United States of America

To Thomas

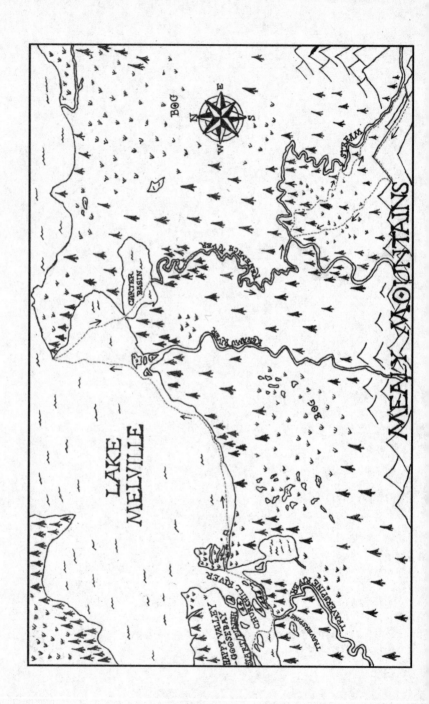

CONTENTS

	Preface	I
1.	Traverspine	3
2.	Where the Wild Things Are	12
3.	The Road to Labrador	19
4.	Into the Wild	27
5.	Clues from the Past	34
6.	Ruins in the Woods	42
7.	It Comes at Night	50
8.	Downriver	62
9.	Into the Fog	73
10.	Legends of Long Ago	82
11.	Against the Current	94
12.	Unknown Things	104
13.	The Land of Shadows	111
14.	Horror in the Woods	121
15.	Crossing the Divide	132
16.	In the Shadow of the Mountain	141
17.	Night Terrors	148
18.	Tracking the Unknown	161
19.	Night on the Mountain	171
20.	Dawn	179
21.	Over the Mountains	194
22.	Monsters of the Wild	205
23.	Across the Marshes	216
24.	Return	223
	Afterword	233
	Acknowledgments	237

PREFACE

Let us probe the silent places, let us seek what luck betide us;
Let us journey to a lonely land I know.
There's a whisper on the night-wind,
there's a star agleam to guide us,
And the Wild is calling, calling . . . let us go.
—Robert Service, "The Call of the Wild," 1907

THE PALE GLOW of the moon, half hidden in clouds, illuminated the ghostly shapes of the crooked black spruces. They were ancient trees, their bark coarse and scaly, their branches draped as if in cobwebs with hanging mosses. We'd camped in the shadows of the mountains, near a nameless stream that tumbled over rocks already half a billion years old before the first dinosaur ever walked the earth. The place had the feel of ancientness about it—as if it had lain undisturbed for centuries.

I lay outstretched in my tent, utterly exhausted from a brutally hard day, almost delirious from dehydration and hundreds of blackfly bites. Obtaining water had proved difficult, as the raging mountain stream, with its crisp, cool waters, lay at the bottom of steep cliffs that were difficult to scale down. Instead we'd found a small, stagnant pool in the swamp woods and drank from it.

I cast a glance out my tent's screen door at the moonlit forest. The stunted spruces and firs had been weirdly shaped and contorted by the mountain gales, and the shadows cast by the moonlight made it difficult to distinguish objects among them. Earlier in the day, while clawing our way through deep thickets that sealed off this isolated mountain valley, we'd come across large bear tracks. At least we thought they were bear tracks, but they hadn't registered very clearly in the mossy ground. In any case the tracks were big, and must have been fresh to have remained imprinted in the moss. They'd led into the valley we were now camped in. I clutched the knife that lay beside my sleeping bag a little tighter.

For a few seconds, lying in the dark in my tent, I thought I heard a faint noise distinct from the creaking of the spruces in the wind, almost like a whispering, strange and unnatural, echoing apparently from the caves higher up the forested slope. I shivered in the cold and craned my ear trying to listen more intently, but the strange sound had ceased—leaving only the creaking of the trees and the sound of the mountain stream tumbling over rocks filling the darkness around me.

TRAVERSPINE

Ghost stories are very real in this land of scattered,
lonely homes and primitive fears . . .
—Elliott Merrick, *True North*, 1933

T RAVERSPINE IS NOT a place you will find on most maps.
A century ago it stood near where the winding course of
the Traverspine River drains down out of little-known mountains in central Labrador. Today it's an abandoned ghost town,
almost all trace of it swallowed up by dark woods that cloak
thousands of square miles.

Labrador was one of the last places in the Western Hemisphere to be inhabited by humans. Partly this was because of its
remote location hidden beyond mountains at the northeast end
of the continent, far from where humans first crossed into North
America from Siberia. It was also owing to its harsh climate and
forbidding landscape, chilled by frigid ocean currents (coastal
Alaska, in contrast, is much more hospitable). The Ice Age, too,
lingered here longer than elsewhere, with enormous glaciers
covering the land. The ancient inhabitants, the Dorset, vanished
long ago, leaving in their wake only deserted campsites.

Encompassing nearly three hundred thousand square kilometres of windswept peaks, forbidding glaciers, dark spruce forests, vast tundra, and towering fjords along its rugged coastline, Labrador even today remains a place of quiet solitudes, where a person can roam for miles without encountering another soul. The total population per square kilometre works out to a minuscule 0.092 people, and most of that is concentrated in just two towns separated by hundreds of kilometres of uninhabited wilderness. If ever there were a lonely land that attracts lonely souls, Labrador is surely it.

Not surprisingly, legends flourish in this remote place where Vikings wandered over a thousand years ago and icebergs the size of castles drift in thick mists just offshore. Deep in Labrador's limitless spruce woods, moving silently as shadows, are living ghosts, the sphinx-like lynx. Meanwhile swollen rivers with dangerous currents snake across the landscape, originating from sources high up in inaccessible mountains—the home of gray wolves, bears, and according to some, things not found in any zoology book. Little wonder then that around dusky campfires old-timers told tales of haunted valleys, unknown tracks, ghostly apparitions, and nameless sounds on the night wind. Local superstition held that in the shadows of the moonlight, flickering lights known as will-o'-the-wisps could lead people astray into trackless muskegs covering hundreds of miles. Hints of some of these legends can be found in the faded pages of old exploration and fur trade records.

My natural affinity has long been for quiet, lonely woods and other wild places. I love wandering for months without coming across a road or town. It's a passion I first developed in childhood exploring the woods that surrounded my family's home, and which I've since managed to turn into a career. By 2019 my wanderings had taken me to nearly every corner of Canada's immense wilderness. I'd rambled among the ancient hills of northern Quebec and Ontario, paddled the subarctic rivers, trudged through the swamps and bogs of the Hudson Bay Lowlands, bounded along ice floes with polar bears in the High Arctic, explored the western mountains, and crossed alone nearly four thousand kilometres of Canada's North. But one place on the map had always somehow managed to elude me— Labrador. That is, until one evening I seemed to find myself caught in a web that drew me to that strange wilderness.

Inevitably, in pursuing such journeys and adventures, I'd heard my share of tall tales and campfire legends. But none ever sent a shiver down my spine quite like the one I stumbled across on that cold winter's evening alone in my study, my desk piled high with old maps and books. I was neck-deep in research to complete a Ph.D. in history from McMaster University, studying some old exploration accounts and fur trade records. My primary focus was on western Canada, but as frequently happens, one reference led to another, and having strayed in my reading, I picked up a curious old volume that concerned Labrador, that wild land of mystery and legend. The story dated back to a time when light came from the flicker of a candle or the blaze of a spruce fire, when a person had to rely on their own strength and wits for survival. In that time and place, most people had little experience of the wider world and access to books or newspapers was a limited luxury, to say nothing of other things our modern world takes for granted.

The story that caught my attention was buried in an otherwise straightforward chronicle by one Elliott Merrick, an American resident of Labrador. Merrick, in an entry dated September 1930, described a chilling tale he'd heard from an old trapper about a place called Traverspine. In the early 1900s this secluded little settlement had been the scene of extraordinary encounters with large creatures none could identify. Strange tracks were found in the woods, unearthly cries were heard in the night, and sled dogs went missing. Children reported encountering a terrifying, grinning animal of large size that stalked them. Families slept with cabin doors barred and axes and guns at their bedsides.

It is perhaps best that I quote Merrick's story in full, so that readers may judge it for themselves:

Ghost stories are very real in this land of scattered, lonely homes and primitive fears. The Traverspine "gorilla" is one of the creepiest. About twenty years ago one of the little girls was playing in an open grassy clearing one autumn afternoon when she saw come out of the woods a huge hairy thing with low-hanging arms. It was about seven feet tall when it stood erect, but sometimes it dropped to all fours. Across the top of its head was a white mane. She said it grinned at her, and she could see its white teeth. When it beckoned to her she ran screaming to the house. Its tracks were everywhere in the mud and sand, and later in the snow. They measured the tracks and cut out paper patterns of them which they still keep. It is a strange-looking foot, about twelve inches long, narrow at the heel and forking at the front into two broad, round-ended toes. Sometimes its print was so deep it looked to weigh five hundred pounds. At other times the beast's mark looked no deeper than a man's track. They set bear traps for it, but it would never go near them. It ripped the bark off trees and rooted up huge rotten logs as though it were looking for grubs. They organized hunts for it, and the lumbermen who were then at Mud Lake came with their rifles and lay out all night by the paths watching, but with no success. A dozen people have told me they saw its track with their own eyes and it was unlike anything ever seen or heard of. One afternoon one of the children saw it peeping in the window. She yelled and old Mrs. Michelin grabbed a gun and ran for the door. She just saw the top of its head disappearing into a clump of willows. She fired where she saw the bushes moving and thinks she wounded it. She says too that it had a ruff of white across the top of its head. At night they used to bar the door with a stout birch beam and all sleep upstairs, taking guns and axes with them. The dogs knew it was there too, for the family would hear them growl and snarl when it approached. Often it must have driven them into the river, for they would be soaking wet in the morning. One night the dogs faced the thing, and it lashed at them with a stick or club, which hit a corner of the house with such force it made the beams tremble. The old man and boys carried guns wherever they went but never got a shot at it. For two winters it was there. They believe to this day it was one of the devil's agents or more likely "the old feller" himself.

Merrick said nothing further about this story, and seems never to have offered any explanation for it. If he questioned the locals' belief that a supernatural being, the devil or one of his "agents," had haunted the isolated settlement, he made no mention of it.

On that first encounter years ago with Merrick's story, it struck me as more interesting and detailed than most supernatural wilderness tales I'd come across—but who was to say Merrick hadn't simply made it all up? After all, in such a remote place, it isn't easy to corroborate such claims. Most wilderness "monster" stories fall into this category: they were made long ago in isolated locales by a single source, far from any other literate observer and with no possibility of cross-referencing them. Initially I assumed this had to be the case with Merrick's story too, so I tried my best to forget about it and return to my other research.

Accounts of strange, unknown tracks and sightings of unidentified animals are part of the folklore of the wilderness, told and retold around countless campfires down through the ages. Canada, with its vast wilderness of primeval forests and thousands of snow-capped mountains, is particularly rich in this kind of lore. I knew my fair share of them: sasquatch stories from the mountains of British Columbia, windigo tales from the limitless subarctic forests, and narratives of other, nameless ones. But most of these seldom seemed very tangible. They usually followed a familiar pattern—the story is vague, the recorder doesn't often claim to have seen the thing themselves, but they say they know someone else who has.

Yet something about the details in Merrick's account—the grinning teeth, the white mane, the peculiar tracks—seared it into my mind. Somehow it seemed more convincing than others I'd come across in old fur trappers' diaries or explorers' journals;

for one thing, there was the alleged physical evidence in the form of tracks that had been carefully recorded. Eventually, my curiosity led me to dig deeper into surviving records of Labrador. On an idle, rainy morning one late summer day, I dug up some old books and historical sources relating to Labrador and spread out an antique map of the territory across my desk. Again, I had little expectation of finding any sources that might substantiate such an extraordinary tale. Almost never in my research on other wilderness legends had I ever succeeded in finding any corroborating reports.

Such was my surprise, then, when I eventually found no fewer than six contemporary accounts by different individuals that recorded in detail the same chilling encounters with strange, unknown creatures in the area around Traverspine a century ago. It seemed there was more to the case after all. Even more surprising was that among these records were one by a wildlife biologist and three by medical doctors.

One of the earliest accounts was made in 1919 by Dr. Wilfred Grenfell, the celebrated Newfoundland physician who'd travelled extensively across Labrador to provide medical care to isolated communities. One of Grenfell's colleagues who worked in the area, Dr. Harry Paddon, believed that the existence of the strange Traverspine beast was "too well-founded to doubt." Another colleague, Dr. C. Hogarth Forsyth, who also spent years travelling the Labrador wilds, described the tracks as "ape-like" and noted that they sometimes "led to nests under trees." This was all highly unusual and intriguing, coming as it did from medical professionals and men of science. Forsyth, like the others, rejected any notion that the tracks could have been made by a bear, noting that they'd been examined by "trappers whose living depends on their knowledge of tracks."

Of the half-dozen chroniclers, only Professor Bruce Wright, a wildlife biologist, made some attempt to explain away the creature. Wright wondered whether it had been a barren-land grizzly, a creature common in the western Arctic but seldom encountered in modern times east of Hudson Bay. However, when he suggested the possibility of its having been a bear to his informants, "they all laughed at that as they were all very familiar with bear tracks." Wright noted of his interview with Mrs. Michelin, the woman who'd seen the creature firsthand and fired at it: "I asked Mrs. Michelin point blank if it could have been a bear. Her response was telling: 'It was no bear Mr. Wright. I have killed twelve bears on my husband's trapline and I know their tracks well. I saw enough of this thing to be sure of that. I fired a shotgun at it and I heard the shot hit.'"

But if it wasn't a bear, which clearly doesn't match the descriptions given, what else could have inspired such terror? The villagers apparently believed that what had plagued them was a creature from the netherworld, a supernatural demon. Native lore spoke of dreaded windigos that haunted the remote regions of Labrador, places even the local Montagnais avoided if they could. But the descriptions given at Traverspine don't seem to match that of a windigo either. Dr. Forsyth speculated that there might be some previously unknown animal—there were, after all, still vast areas of uncharted wilderness in the early 1900s, as well as animal species unknown to science, among them the spirit bear of the British Columbian rainforest, which had long been dismissed as a myth. Modern skeptics might be inclined to think it all an elaborate hoax, or merely the figments of overwrought imaginations stressed by the isolation of life in subarctic Labrador. But I don't think this is the case.

Unlike many sasquatch or "bigfoot" sightings, the Labrador accounts can't be so easily written off as mere campfire tales. The multiple sightings, the dogs driven to frenzy, and the dozens of eyewitness reports of tracks that were not only minutely examined but carefully preserved seem to speak to something more real. It's also frightening—there seems to have been hostile intent on the part of the creature, whatever it was. The accounts all mention missing dogs, enormous tracks, and the targeting of children. Finally, there was the specific rejection of any notion that it could have been a bear by persons well qualified to judge.

Reading the passages I'd unearthed, my mind fixated on that mysterious place on the old map, Traverspine, and the little-known mountains that surrounded it. Gradually, as I accumulated more and more evidence that the skeptical side of me couldn't quite dismiss, I found myself, almost against my better judgment, leaning toward the possibility that something terrifying really did plague that isolated place.

I decided to investigate further. There was only so much I could glean from old accounts. Tracing my fingers across the faded map, I resolved to set off for Labrador to see if I could find the ruins of Traverspine—if any such ruins should exist—and from there, plunge into the surrounding mountains.

2

WHERE THE WILD THINGS ARE

It is a suggestive fact that the great peninsula of Labrador, although probably the first part of the American mainland to be seen by Europeans, contains to-day the largest unexplored area on the Western Continent.
—Henry Bryant, *A Journey to the Grand Falls of Labrador*, 1894

A S IT HAPPENED, I'd just spent a month alone in the wilderness on an expedition for the Royal Canadian Geographical Society in the Hudson Bay Lowlands, and although it was now late summer, I figured if I wasted no time, I might get to Labrador before winter set in. I mostly do solo journeys, but for this one, a partner seemed a prudent idea. Not so much because I worried about anything strange, but rather because the rough plan I'd drawn up entailed some pretty hazardous canoeing late in the season on an inland arm of the North Atlantic Ocean. So I concluded finding a partner was the responsible thing to do.

But oddly enough, it turned out that on such short notice there were few people I knew who would willingly commit to such a venture. I did have one acquaintance who came to mind; he was a staunch believer in sasquatch and other cryptids (animals unrecognized by science) and also an amateur ghost

hunter named Graham. Knowing his interest in any supernatural or unusual subject, I sent him some of the accounts I'd
found concerning Labrador. Getting his opinion on the matter
might prove valuable.

Graham's response, after having carefully reviewed the
documents I'd sent, was that he found the whole thing rather
terrifying and mysterious. He thought the accounts didn't match
a sasquatch—the geographic area was all wrong. Nevertheless,
he believed that the story recounted by Merrick in the 1930s
had, in his words, "the ring of truth to it." Graham felt that
what I was dealing with in Traverspine wasn't an animal at all,
but rather a demon or something else supernatural. He went on
to inform me that under no circumstances would he wish to go
wandering about in the wilderness there, and advised me that
my plans to do so were most imprudent.

Graham's warning failed to deter me. Only it seemed as if
I would be out of luck in finding an expedition partner. I ran
through my list of acquaintances and companions—one after
another, there was some objection or prior commitment that
ruled them out. My old friend Wes, a stalwart companion on
past adventures, had his hands full juggling numerous jobs as a
self-employed contractor.

In despair, my mind drawing blanks, I pushed aside the
exploration records that had monopolized my desk and pulled
down an old school yearbook. Leafing through the pages
absent-mindedly, I wondered what had become of many of my
old classmates. More importantly, were there any who might
have a sudden wish to plunge into the Labrador wilderness to
chase after a Traverspine gorilla?

That's when it hit me—*I knew the perfect person for just such an undertaking.* Or in any case, someone who'd do in a pinch. His name was Zach. We'd gone to school together, although he'd been a year ahead of me and we hadn't been friends. But I'd crossed paths with him from time to time at the local hockey rink and knew him to be tough-minded, physically active, and an avid outdoorsperson, especially where fishing was concerned. He'd grown up on a dairy farm, worked at a scrap yard, and run unsuccessfully for mayor in our hometown (the mayor's job was now occupied by his father, a retired farmer, who still grew some corn and soybeans). In fact, rumour had it he'd taken up fighting for money in addition to his day job (in insurance). Surely, if ever there were a person exceedingly qualified for an expedition, it was Zach.

I took the liberty of sending him an immediate text message. I figured it wouldn't do to beat about the bush, so I cut right to things: "Hey Zach. Super short notice, but would you want to go on an expedition to Labrador? Objective is to explore a haunted river, find any trace of a ghost settlement, and climb some mountains etc. We would leave Tuesday (most likely) and be gone at least several weeks."

I wasn't sure what kind of response such a message would elicit, but my advice is that whenever you're planning an expedition to investigate a supernatural beast, always take the direct approach. A response came back nine minutes later:

"How much would this cost?"

That was an encouraging sign, the mark of a sensible person—exactly the kind of partner such an expedition required. I assured him it wouldn't cost him a thing, at least financially.

After that crucial matter had been satisfied, it took only three minutes for Zach to send his next message: "Ok, I'm 95% in, just need to convince pregnant wife that this is ok. I'll call you when the meeting I'm in is done and I've talked to her."

He was proving to be a very prudent person. True to his word, Zach called me a short time later. He asked only a few questions. I told him we'd have to be ready to leave within seventy-two hours; that he'd have to meet me on Tuesday morning in the driveway of my home in Norfolk County near Lake Erie *at seven a.m. sharp* (or at any rate not later than eight or nine), and that from there, we'd drive approximately thirty-two hours to Labrador. Once we reached our destination, we'd leave our vehicle behind, load up a canoe, and set off into the wild. He agreed with all of this. And just like that, our expedition was a go.

I sent Zach a list of some of the gear he'd have to round up: backpack, tent, life jacket, emergency blanket, two sets of clothing, waterproof bags, waders (for walking upstream on rivers), sleeping bag and sleeping pad, first-aid kit, warm gloves, garlic, silver bullets, and a few other typical camping items. I also sent him my notes and the clippings I'd dug up about the Traverspine mystery. I wanted to get his opinion on them and see if he had any theories.

Meanwhile, I busied myself packing my own gear: three paddles, the canoe, a life jacket, some leftover dried food rations and granola bars, a watertight barrel to store them in, a Swiss Army knife, a significantly larger knife, a hatchet, warm clothing, a stainless-steel pot for cooking, a compass, a flashlight, and some paracord. I also packed a huge amount of photocopied material consisting of primary source documents from Labrador's history, and plenty of spare batteries so that I'd be able to read them in my tent at night.

Then I went outside to our garden where my wife, Alexandria, was busy pruning some branches. She's an avid gardener and crafter, a lover of plants and birds, although she doesn't exactly share my passion for adventures and expeditions. We were recently married and had relocated from northern Ontario to Norfolk County, on Lake Erie's north shore, a place I found congenial given its old-growth forests. We enjoyed our life in the countryside, surrounded by woods and fields.

"I'm leaving on an expedition to Labrador to search for the ruins of an abandoned settlement where some sort of monster haunted it a hundred years ago," I said.

She nodded as if she'd expected as much, without looking up from her gardening work.

"I'm leaving Tuesday and I'll likely be gone for several weeks," I added.

"Who are you going with?" she asked, still focused on the shrubs.

"Zach," I said.

She looked up for the first time from her gardening. "Zach who?"

"Zach the mixed martial arts guy."

"Have you ever been camping with him before?"

"No," I said.

She nodded. "Okay, well I'm sure that will work out fine."

—

Three days passed quickly, and Zach arrived on schedule. He stood about six foot two, lean and wiry from triathlon training and mixed martial arts, thirty-five years of age, bearded and chewing tobacco. After losing his bid for the mayor's office, he'd taken up fighting for money, a common enough career path. He'd trained in Brazilian jiujitsu and had become a professional MMA fighter. Zach had won several of his bouts by knockouts and another by submission (he broke his opponent's arm). Luckily he was between fights at the moment. Even-tempered, level-headed, and keenly interested in the natural world, he'd make an excellent canoe partner, I figured, though I'd never spent any significant amount of time with him.

For our twenty-five-hundred-kilometre road trip, we'd decided to take his vehicle, a 2014 Mazda CX-5 crossover SUV. We strapped my fifteen-foot Nova Craft canoe onto it. This was the same canoe that had crossed Canada's Arctic with me, and although it was designed as primarily a solo canoe, I regarded it as my best friend and had no doubt it would serve us well. Our other gear we stashed in the back: paddles, life jackets, backpacks, and the watertight barrel with the food rations. We also had a couple of motion-activated trail cameras for setting up around our camps at night. One of these was mine, and the other had been loaned to us by a friend of Zach's who happened to be a wildlife biologist with the Canadian Wildlife Service.

With that, we bid farewell. Our route took us east through southern Ontario and then into southern Quebec, following the St. Lawrence River. We passed through Montreal and

Quebec City and then continued along the St. Lawrence, passing beneath the shadows of the Laurentian Mountains. For much of our long drive, my mind was lost in my thoughts, my head crammed with visions of Labrador and its strange legends.

3

THE ROAD TO LABRADOR

On this dim verge of the known world there were other perils
than those of the waves . . . Griffins—so ran the story—
infested the mountains of Labrador.
—Francis Parkman, *Pioneers of France in the New World*, 1865

M ISTY MOUNTAINS HEMMED in the narrow, winding
roadway. The day had dawned cold and clear, but as we'd
left the last city behind on the Gulf of St. Lawrence and entered
deeper into the wilderness, the skies had darkened ominously.
A drizzling rain was now falling, with fierce gusts howling down
from the surrounding mountains. For the past seven hours we
hadn't passed a single town of any kind.

We were driving north on Quebec's isolated Route 389,
which winds like a thin gravel ribbon nearly six hundred kilometres through mountainous wilderness to the border of Labrador.
It's one of the longest unserviced stretches of road anywhere in
North America. Much of it is rough, unpaved, and completely
out of reach of cell service. Opened in 1987, the road's purpose
was to link the little mining town of Fermont on the Labrador
border with the settlements of the Gulf of St. Lawrence.

The drizzle now turned to a lashing rain and the wind grew fiercer, shaking the car and the canoe strapped on its roof. Around us the mountains rose to heights of over three thousand feet, their ancient summits concealed in thick mists. The whole landscape had a wild and forlorn character, which made it easy to see how such a place could breed legends.

Geographers of the 1500s had believed that the mountains of Labrador were the haunt of griffins and other monsters. Navigators could be forgiven for thinking so; from the heavy seas of the North Atlantic, amid icebergs and thick fogs, the looming mountains of the bleak Labrador shore certainly did look like the kind of place where a griffin or dragon might live. On faded maps from this same era, one finds marked just off the southern tip of Labrador the ominously named "Isles de Demons," phantom islands that were thought to be infested with all manner of monsters.

In 1534 the French explorer Jacques Cartier, upon his first glimpse of the forbidding mountains that rise like a dark barrier along the Labrador coast, confided in his diary, "I am rather inclined to believe this is the land God gave to Cain." He felt that the barren mountains were cursed. These rugged mountains are among the oldest on earth and extend northward for hundreds of miles, all the way to northernmost Labrador, where at the tip of the continent they reach their icy apex in the Torngat Mountains. Here in this remote corner of Canada, the Torngats form some of the highest peaks east of the Rockies in mainland North America. The name itself, Torngats, is derived from an Inuit word meaning "place of evil spirits."

The Inuit had a tradition that this mysterious and unknown land was inhabited by not just evil spirits but giants. The Inuit, according to both oral history and archaeology, avoided Labrador until the 1500s, when a few hardy wayfarers crossed over the ice from the north on Baffin Island, a hazardous undertaking. The Inuit myths described the creatures they found inhabiting Labrador as ogre-like subhumans, incredibly strong and large but slow-witted and primitive. Some anthropologists have speculated that these legends were based on actual encounters with the Dorset, a mysterious people who lived in the Canadian Arctic before the Inuit arrived from Siberia. The Indigenous Naskapi and Montagnais, members of the great Algonquian nations that ranged to the south across the boreal forest, also thought there was something strange about the mountains and forests of Labrador. Around shared campfires they spoke of supernatural beings that stalked the deepest depths of the northern wilderness: the cannibalistic Atchen and dreaded windigo, as well as mysterious creatures that dwelled in mountain caves and could play tricks on humans. Of all the supernatural beings found in Algonquian legends, windigos were the most terrifying. It was whispered that they were giant monsters that hungered for human flesh. Those foolhardy enough to wander the wilds alone, especially in winter, were believed to be the most likely victims.

Nor were these the only groups who looked upon the northern mountains and spruce forests that extended into Labrador with superstitious forebodings. A thousand years ago, to the Vikings, Labrador, or "Markland" as they called it, with its mist-shrouded mountains and deep fjords, was a land where terrifying frost giants and other strange creatures lurked. For centuries the Vikings had made dangerous voyages through the icy seas of the North Atlantic to Labrador's rugged coastline. What had tempted them to risk such perils to reach this land of legend? For a northern people, it was that most precious of all commodities: wood. The Vikings needed Labrador for its abundant supplies of lumber, which they lacked in their harsh Greenlandic homelands. But beyond the windswept beaches and rocky coves only the bravest Norse warriors dared venture. One of the ancient Vinland sagas, the oldest written account of what is now Labrador, tells the tale of the Norse wayfarer Thorvald, a son of Erik the Red, who, it was said, was killed while exploring Labrador by a bizarre one-legged monster known as a uniped. Clearly, these were mysterious lands where legends had long flourished.

—

We reached the mining town of Fermont after a nine-hour drive from the south along the snaking road. Our first glimpse of this company town, built to mine the rich deposits of iron ore nearby, was of a bleak, desolate place in the midst of vast subarctic forests. The mine itself, situated on the outskirts of the settlement, reminded me of Mordor, an impression perhaps enhanced by the dark, overcast skies, howling wind, and steady rain. The surrounding mountains were denuded of all vegetation, leaving the barren slopes looking like a kind of moonscape. A vast complex of pits, unpaved roads, gravel hills, and industrial infrastructure unfolded before us; haul trucks moved rubble about while great steel structures rose above the darkened landscape. Dynamite had blasted out an enormous, gaping chasm in the earth. The waters of an adjacent lake, in contrast to the clear blue waters of the lakes we'd passed on the road, were a reddish colour, a result of runoff from the mining operations.

We spent the night in Fermont at the only hotel in town, which is part of a huge interconnected building complex that doubles as a wind-break for the town. The whole area is one of the windiest inhabited places in Canada, whipped by fierce winds and bitterly cold temperatures for much of the year. There isn't much in the way of restaurants or cafés in Fermont, which exists almost solely as a mining town.

By five the next morning we were on the road again, passing from Quebec into Labrador. Just outside Fermont, on the Labrador side of the invisible border, sits Labrador City, a bigger town with a range of services. But Zach and I were eager to be on our way: it was already September 3, with the first hints of winter not far off. So for breakfast we ate packed apples and granola bars and just kept driving.

The lonely road we'd been following, one that sees little traffic besides the occasional logging truck or mine worker, becomes the Trans-Labrador Highway after snaking across the provincial border. Opened in 1992, the road stretches nearly twelve hundred kilometres through the Labrador wilderness, linking the handful of tiny settlements. For the most part, as we found driving along it with barely a sight of another vehicle, the road remains the domain of wandering timber wolves, foxes, black bears, and boreal owls. To its south is the Churchill River, previously called the Grand River, a once mighty waterway diverted in the 1960s as part of a massive hydroelectric project. As we drove along, in places huge hydro lines were visible, which, surrounded by otherwise undisturbed subarctic forest, had the look of a sort of science fiction creation plopped down on a distant planet.

The long drive, about thirty-two hours all told from when we'd left my place in Norfolk County, gave Zach and me plenty of time to discuss matters. Neither of us believed in sasquatch; nor did we trouble ourselves too much with thoughts of demons. But I was willing to allow that the world was a vast place, containing many mysterious and odd things, some of them perhaps outside the bounds of current scientific understanding. This feeling was accentuated by our surroundings; the road was but a tiny, narrow ribbon in the midst of a sea of sombre spruces and tamaracks, which even today undoubtedly hid places no human foot had ever trod.

I asked Zach whether, having examined the descriptions I'd sent him about Traverspine, he had any initial theories. He suggested that the "monster" might in fact have been a polar bear suffering from mange, a skin disease caused by parasitic mites that occasionally afflicts both wild and domestic animals. The mange, if left untreated, can cause the animal's fur to fall out. In recent years, mange outbreaks have been quite common among black bears in the eastern United States; we'd both seen photos of black bears afflicted with mange that gave them a very bizarre, almost humanoid appearance. I'd also read of at least a few cases among polar bears. Moreover, polar bears, as an adaptation to their cold environments, actually have black skin beneath their fur. So an emaciated polar bear whose fur had fallen out would look quite unrecognizable, particularly in an environment the bears aren't normally associated with such as the spruce woods of interior Labrador. As Zach elaborated, a polar bear with mange would appear vaguely ape-like, especially in uncertain light or when half concealed in willow bushes, and in desperation it might be tempted to come around people's houses. The white blaze or mane mentioned in several of the accounts, moreover, could be explained as remnant fur around the scruff of the bear's neck—the last spot where mange would cause it to fall out from furious scratching.

Zach added some other observations: a bear would align well with the description of the creature alternating from moving on four legs to two, as well as ripping up old logs as if looking for grubs, something a bear might well do. As well, Dr. Forsyth, in his account, mentioned the tracks leading across ice, a natural route for a polar bear to take. I agreed that this wasn't a bad hypothesis.

A bigger question, though, was whether a polar bear would venture as far inland as Traverspine. Normally, polar bears are found on ice floes or along the sea coast, since the majority of their diet is made up of seals. They do, however, wander into the mountains of Labrador, especially in early fall when the sea ice has mostly melted. Pregnant females in particular are known to range much farther inland when looking for a den site. I turned to my historical sources to see whether I could find any hint of polar bears ever making it as far inland as the western end of Lake Melville—which is not, strictly speaking, a lake at all, but rather an extension of Hamilton Inlet, an inland arm of the North Atlantic Ocean that cuts into Labrador's eastern coast.

Merrick hadn't made any mention of polar bears inland in his memoirs, nor had most of the fur trade sources I'd read.

But flipping through my copious photocopies of old sources, I found something intriguing in an 1896 report by Albert Peter Low, who'd worked for the Geological Survey of Canada. Low's official report of the survey work he did in Labrador between 1892 and 1895 contained this detail: "During the winter of 1894 the tracks of three white bears were seen close to Northwest River, at the head of Hamilton Inlet, and a few specimens have been killed in that locality." Northwest River is less than thirty kilometres from Traverspine. So a wandering polar bear, perhaps especially one afflicted with mange, could indeed find its way to the Traverspine River.

Zach's polar bear mange theory provided us with a working hypothesis, but there were also some strong points against it. It didn't explain the tracks, and it didn't explain how there could be two animals, something several of the accounts mention in considerable detail, implying that there was both a male and a smaller female. Even if we were to discount that aspect, it also doesn't explain avoiding baited traps (a mangy bear would be desperate for food). In particular, the trappers and lumberjacks would almost certainly have recognized polar bear tracks for what they were. Ultimately then, these objections forced us to rule out this theory.

Whatever had terrified that place long ago must have been something else.

4

INTO THE WILD

Now, brothers, for the icebergs
Of frozen Labrador,
Floating spectral in the moonshine,
Along the low, black shore!
—John Greenleaf Whittier, "The Fishermen," 1850

JUST PAST NOON, having driven nearly six hundred kilometres east from Fermont, we arrived at what for us was the end of the line: the modern town of Happy Valley-Goose Bay. The town sits on the north bank of the Churchill River, where it empties into Lake Melville. The heavy rain of the night before had ceased, but the wind remained as fierce as ever and the skies overcast, with big, billowing clouds blowing rapidly by as we drove down the main street. The town had sprung into existence during the height of World War II, when it was determined by the Allies that an air base should be constructed in Labrador to defend the North Atlantic and as a refuelling stop for military aircraft headed to Europe. The air base was built at Goose Bay, with a small civilian settlement founded nearby in Happy Valley. At one point the base was home to air forces from many Allied nations, but after the end of the Cold War only a limited number of personnel remained. In the early 1970s Happy Valley and Goose Bay amalgamated, becoming the hyphenated Happy Valley-Goose Bay of today. With a population of about eight thousand, it's the largest town in Labrador.

We pulled into a conservation area on the outskirts of town, driving along a dirt road through spruce woods down to a small gravel parking lot along the river. Zach dropped me off with the canoe and other gear, while he returned to town. The plan was to leave his car there, and then he'd walk back and join me. Although it occurred to me as I stood alone in the parking lot watching Zach drive off down the dusty road that he could, if he got cold feet or had second thoughts, just drive away and leave me here on my own.

At any rate, I set myself to hauling the canoe and gear down to the sandy riverbank. From the bank, I had a magnificent view of the mighty Churchill River and the dark mountains that rose in the distance beyond it. The river here was nearly a kilometre and a half wide, with a muddy brown colour to its waters and a maze of sand flats that reminded me of the Mackenzie River in the Northwest Territories. The fierce wind, coming from the west, was bitter and cold, and whipped the middle of the vast river into whitecaps. Under normal circumstances I wouldn't want to paddle a fifteen-foot canoe across such a wide expanse, given the wind and current. But I was eager to be off. So I started loading the canoe, carefully feeling the weight of each pack and judging where best to put it.

As I did so I became aware that another vehicle, a Ford pickup truck, had rumbled into the parking lot above the sandbank and parked there. The man in the driver's seat sat watching me down below. I could guess his thoughts: *Who is crazy and reckless enough to set off in this wind in a canoe on the Churchill River in September?*

The paddles and life jackets were still in the parking lot, and I returned to fetch them. As I did so, the man in the truck, who looked to be about sixty, rolled down his window and waved a hand at me.

"Going canoeing?" he asked.

"Yes," I replied, picking up the paddles.

"For work or pleasure?" He seemed to be sizing me up.

"Both," I said.

"You a surveyor?"

"Not exactly," I replied.

"You're all by yourself?" he asked.

"My friend will be here any minute," I said, casting a glance back up the dirt road for any sign of Zach. There was none.

"Where you headed?"

"Across the river"—I gestured toward the distant mountains—"to the Traverspine River."

"You'll never make it there." He shook his head. "That canoe," he said, pointing at it dismissively, "won't make it across. You'll end up way out in Lake Melville with this wind and current."

"We'll be fine," I assured him. In truth, I was a little concerned about the wind gusts and whitecaps, but I thought it best not to show it.

He shook his head again. "That little canoe won't make it across. You don't think the wind is bad here on shore, but

I'll tell you, you get out there in the middle of that river"—he nodded confidently—"it'll feel ten times as strong. You see those waves? Believe me, they'll swallow you up."

I tried to win him over with levity. "Well, that's okay," I said, "I could use a bath. I've been in a car three days straight."

The stranger only shook his head disapprovingly.

"You got a satellite phone? Bears are awful hungry this time of year."

I nodded.

"That wilderness out there, it's a rough country. Easy to get lost in. No one will ever find you. There's places out there that nobody's ever set foot in. Traverspine River isn't a smart place to be heading," he pronounced solemnly.

Just then Zach finally appeared; I wondered what had taken him so long.

"Here comes my friend," I said, gesturing to Zach.

The man glanced out his window as if he half doubted I really had a companion. But then seeing Zach, who was clad in a wide-brimmed leather hat with a knife on his belt, he quieted down.

I thanked the man for his advice. He nodded before rolling up his window and driving off.

"What did that guy say?" asked Zach as he strode up to me.

"Oh," I said, looking down at the canoe, "just that it sounds like we'll have a lovely outing."

Zach nodded.

We finished our packing and switched into our wading boots. I didn't doubt that a careless attempt to cross the river could end badly. The ferocious wind gusts and strong current called for a careful plan.

Rather than simply blundering out straight across the wide expanse of open river, which would, if we didn't capsize, cause the current and wind to carry us far downstream from where we needed to reach, Zach and I thought up a different approach. We'd instead hug the near shore, tucking out of the worst of the wind along the willow-clad banks, and from there we'd paddle up a small channel that snaked around behind the mud flats. Following it would screen us from the winds and enable us to get upstream of our objective: the mouth of the Traverspine River on the far side. On the downside, to accomplish this we'd have to paddle head-on against the river's powerful current. But not for nothing had I recruited Zach. I figured our combined strength would be enough to overcome the swirling current. Once we reached the end of the narrow channel, we'd be into the wide-open river. But instead of trying to beeline it straight for the far shore, exposing the canoe broadside to the wind gusts, we'd point our bow upstream and angle across diagonally. This would compensate for the force of the current, and by angling our nose into the wind, we'd be much less exposed.

Our plans made, we waded into the muddy water along the sandbank. I cast a last glance across the river at the distant mountains. "Any second thoughts?" I asked.

"We didn't drive thirty-two hours to turn back now," said Zach.

"Right, let's do this."

With that we shoved off. Zach crouched in the bow while I was on my knees in the stern. The river swirled past us, but our strong, determined strokes overcame it. We made better progress than I'd hoped, quickly reaching the end of the sheltered channel formed by the sand flats. Now we had to strike out from shore, facing the full force of the wind.

I paddled hard, straining my muscles and angling the canoe toward the wind and current, thereby making us more aerodynamic and avoiding the gusts hitting us broadside. Zach, meanwhile, was paddling furiously in the front with strong, powerful strokes. The howling wind tossed spray in our faces and kicked up sand. The blowing sand made it difficult to see; it was impossible to make out any openings on the distant shore, which appeared as a blur of green spruces. But somewhere over there, concealed in those woods, was the Traverspine River.

We kept up a hard paddle, keeping the canoe angled into the wind, gradually working ourselves farther from shore. As we neared the middle of the river—over half a kilometre from land—things got a little nerve-racking. Tipping here would be bad. Just then a tremendous gust struck the canoe, pushing us sideways precariously.

"Holy cow!" shouted Zach, swinging his paddle to steady the canoe. "Who knew the wind would be this bad out in the middle?"

"Let's just let the wind turn us," I shouted back over the gusts.

We'd passed the halfway point, which meant we could start angling toward the far bank. Pivoting like this put us out of immediate danger of capsizing, but our relief from battling the wind proved short-lived. The roaring gusts now caught us from behind, making steering difficult. It turned out that I hadn't placed enough weight in the stern behind my seat, and with it sitting slightly higher in the water, it acted almost as a sail catching the wind and making us career wildly about.

Ahead loomed mud flats, where the surf was breaking. There appeared to be a channel snaking through them, which with any luck might lead us to the far shore and out of the wind. I shouted over the gusts to Zach that we'd head for what seemed like a small channel.

He nodded and together we paddled hard. As we neared the mud flat, the water became too shallow to paddle, forcing us to jab off the bottom through breaking surf. Still, we managed to squeeze into the channel, where it was a bit deeper, then force our way through it. The channel led us to deeper water on the other side, just as I'd hoped it would. Now, for the first time, we could make out a gap in the spruces on the far shore—that, I guessed, must be the Traverspine River's mouth. We'd come out just upstream of it. More strenuous paddling at last brought us alongside it, where we were able to tuck in and escape the wind's wrath.

We'd made it.

5

CLUES FROM THE PAST

For three days they sailed with the wind from the south-west until they saw a third land. This land had high mountains, capped by a glacier.
—The Saga of the Greenlanders, circa thirteenth-century AD

THE TRAVERSPINE RIVER loomed into view with inky black water framed by dark spruce woods, quietly flowing down from little-known mountains. We paddled into the river's mouth, freed now from the fierce winds of the Churchill's open expanse. Heaped up on the bank closest to us was a maze of driftwood and dead spruces, while the forest behind appeared so thickly wooded as to be almost impenetrable. The far bank was swampier, but with an equally uninviting thicket of willows and alders. In between, in the river's mouth, stood a low-lying, alder-covered island. There was no sign we could see of any human-made structures.

The settlement of Traverspine had existed somewhere near the river's mouth, though I wasn't sure of the exact location, and the thick woods made guessing difficult. My supposition was that if any ruins were to be found, they'd most likely be on the river's western bank, as it appeared better elevated and less swampy than the woods on the eastern shore. But with the whole area thickly overgrown in a wild tangle of alders, spruces, and firs, searching even the tiniest area for clues would be no easy matter.

In 1894 the surveyor Albert Peter Low had visited Traverspine and briefly described it in his report, but his statement provided few clues to the exact whereabouts of the settlement:

> . . . a small stream, called Traverspine River flows in; it rises in the mountains to the southward. Where this stream discharges into the river, there is a small trading establishment, and the proprietor, Jos[eph] Michelin, has made a little clearing about the place, where he grows an abundant crop of potatoes.

Low's report didn't specify which side of the river the settlement was on nor how far inland it had been. But we guessed the western bank and went ashore to investigate.

Taking a paddle as a walking stick, I led the way into the gloom of the black spruces. Hanging black moss cloaked the trees like cobwebs, while the spruces' dead, claw-like branches barred the way forward, snagging our clothing as we tried to advance. Beneath our feet extended a carpet of green sphagnum moss and bright red bunchberries (which are edible but not very tasty).

Nearby a big spruce had partly toppled over, so I figured I'd climb it to gain a better view of what lay around us. I was hoping to spot some decaying ruins of an old house poking through the spruces, or perhaps the weathered timbers of a collapsed roof.

But I saw nothing encouraging, merely a dense thicket in all directions. If anything had ever existed here, the forest had long since swallowed up all trace of it.

"Hmm, I think we should try searching somewhere else," I said.

"Excellent idea," replied Zach. "So far we've covered at least a quarter of an acre—how much more can there be to search?"

We retraced our steps through the woods back to the canoe. The forest's undergrowth was so thick it would be easy to lose one's way, but fortunately we'd paid careful attention to our surroundings, remembering distinct trees like the odd birch that stood out amid the black spruce. Once back on shore, we relaunched the canoe and headed farther upstream, scrutinizing the wooded banks for any vague hint of a clearing where something might once have existed.

"It looks a bit less thick up there," said Zach from the bow, pointing to an area on the right bank.

We landed the canoe beside it, climbing over dead logs to reach the willowy shore. A muddy embankment led us back into the shadows of the forest, where dead trees creaked noisily in the wind as we spread out and inspected every nook for clues. At one point I spotted a small, weathered wooden box that had been nailed to a balsam fir. It looked almost like a birdhouse, but I recognized it from my time in the Yukon as a trap for pine martens, a weasel-like animal that lives in trees and eats red squirrels. The trap, however, wasn't old enough to be from Traverspine—it seemed to date back only a few decades.

We pushed deeper into the woods until we noticed a skull lying on the ground. There was still a bit of decayed flesh on it.

I knelt down and picked it up, turning it over in my hand to inspect it. "Looks like a fox skull," I concluded.

"Eww, I can't believe you picked that up in your bare hand," said Zach, spitting some tobacco juice out.

"Well, I wanted to be sure it wasn't the skull of an infant sasquatch."

We hiked farther, pushing through clawing branches and weaving around thorn thickets. Then the woods opened up a little and we suddenly found ourselves on the edge of a swamp of alders and willows. Growing alongside the swamp were strawberries and lingonberries, also known as mountain cranberries. We paused our search to snack on some. (After touching the decomposing skull, I used some hand sanitizer I'd luckily stashed in my pocket. My advice is to always carry some when you're looking for ruins, as you can never be sure if you'll have to touch rotting carcasses.) Most of the berries, however, seemed to have already been picked over by black bears.

After a few minutes crouching on our knees picking berries, I came across something. "Look over here," I said, motioning to Zach.

He came up beside me and I pointed at a patch of mud, where large, fresh tracks were clearly imprinted, with claw marks and a footprint that looked half human. "Bear tracks," I said.

Zach nodded. The tracks led on for a few yards before disappearing into some bushy willow. But there was still no sign of any ruins.

"Let's split up," I said.

"Makes perfect sense," nodded Zach.

Zach headed toward some tall black spruces while I approached a chest-high thicket of raspberries. I figured a raspberry thicket could indicate a former clearing where a building might have stood, since raspberries flourish in open sunlight. Plus I was still hungry, and they looked quite tasty.

Nearing the thicket, I noticed more bear tracks, and some very fresh bear droppings of an uncommonly large size. The bear, evidently, had been stuffing itself on raspberries and lingonberries. In my pocket I'd also stashed a bear banger—essentially a firecracker meant to scare off a bear by the sound of the bang (although in my experience it doesn't always work as intended). Grasping the paddle in my hands a little tighter, I entered into the thicket. I didn't wish to blunder into a bear, but on the other hand, the thicket looked too promising a location to pass up.

Avoiding some spiderwebs, I pushed my way deeper in. Concealed beneath the tangle of raspberry bushes was plenty of deadfall, mostly spruces toppled over by strong winds. It allowed me to move a little more freely, as I could balance on the dead tree trunks and tiptoe along. Strangely, I had the vague, uneasy feeling one gets of being watched—as if there were eyes unseen in the bushes all around me. I felt a bear was probably somewhere nearby, or at any rate at least a squirrel. I circled round the thicket, creeping about and looking for any sign of human disturbance.

Suddenly my concentration was broken by a flash of movement over my left shoulder. I spun around and saw a black shape moving through the spruces—a bear! I began to raise my paddle in self-defence, but then I realized it was only a big raven. The bird unleashed a few "caws!" that seemed suspiciously as though it was laughing at me, before flying off in the direction of the river.

"Hmm . . . very atmospheric," I muttered to myself. I decided to return to the swamp and find Zach.

He was crouching in some alders with his back to me when I stumbled out of the thicket.

"See anything?" I asked.

"More bear tracks, but no ruins or anything else," he replied.

"Well, let's head back to the canoe," I said.

Zach and I retraced our steps through the thick woods to where we'd tied up the canoe; once there, we decided to explore the opposite bank, to see if anything might be found in that direction. As we canoed across the river the silence was disturbed by the shrieks of a lone osprey soaring overhead. It seemed to regard us with an air of disdain before disappearing beyond the trees. The opposite bank, it turned out, was little more than a swampy alder thicket. There was again no sign of any ruins or human habitation. After a short while we again returned to the canoe.

"Let's stop on that island in the river's mouth," I suggested. "That'll give me a chance to look over some of my notes and maybe find some clue from one of the old sources that might give us a better idea of where Traverspine once stood."

"Sounds good," nodded Zach from his perch in the canoe's bow. "While we're at it I'll see if I can catch a fish for dinner."

When we landed on the alder-covered island we found more fresh bear tracks as well as moose tracks. Zach busied himself with fishing while I dug out from the watertight barrel my stash of photocopied sources. Most, like Low's, were vague on the whereabouts of Traverspine, alluding only to its location near the mouth of the river without specifics. Flipping through the pages, though, I came upon Elliott Merrick's memoir. He'd been quite specific in his account of what he called the "Traverspine Gorilla," and I wondered if he might have more clues to offer.

"Aha!" I said to Zach, who was just about to cast. "I've got it." Zach looked over.

"Listen to this," I said, and then read aloud from Merrick's memoir:

> A little after noon we were at Traverspine, where we spent the night. It is a narrow river flowing into Grand River, and near the mouth, perched on a high sand bank, are three houses. One belongs to John's father, Uncle Jo, and the other two to his half-brothers, Robert and Jim. A lonely place, but splendid for ducks and geese, partridge, rabbits, porcupine, bear, salmon, trout, and fur. That is why they live here.

The key part of the passage were the words "perched on a high sand bank." Though it might not seem like much, that was the kind of crucial clue we needed. There were no high sandbanks anywhere around us—just low-lying ground. But in the distance, a few hundred metres upriver on the right side, we could see what looked very much like a high sand bank, partially overgrown with alders. Logically, the settlement couldn't have been any farther upriver than that, since it would have been essential for it to command a view of the Grand (Churchill) River. And since there was nothing else within view, I felt that must be the place.

Zach and I hastily relaunched the canoe and paddled upstream toward the alder-covered high bank. I felt tense with anticipation; reading the accounts and staring at the old maps, I'd tried to visualize this place, and now we seemed on the verge of finding it. We beached the canoe, pulled it up securely, then with paddles as walking sticks, ascended the bank along what appeared to be a faint animal trail. It wound up an overgrown hill beneath some spruces and birches.

When we reached the crest of the hill, we found ourselves emerging into a clearing with shoulder-high purple fireweed and trembling aspen saplings, their heart-shaped leaves fluttering in the breeze.

"This looks promising," I whispered excitedly.

"Indeed," said Zach.

We pushed into the clearing, moving silently through the aspens and fireweed. Ahead, on the edge of the forest, loomed the crumbling ruins of a two-storey wood house.

6

RUINS IN THE WOODS

From out the gloom sails the silv'ry moon
O'er forests dark and still
—J.D. Edgar, "Canadian Camping Song," 1893

THE OLD HOUSE HAD partially collapsed and was rather eerie looking in the fading light with its weathered boards. The sun was beginning to set, but we made the most of the remaining light to explore the site. As far as structures went, only the ruins of a single house remained. The structure was too decayed and collapsed to safely enter, but I crept through the high weeds up to the edge of it and peered through one of the window frames.

In the dimly lit interior I could see debris and wood boards strewn about, but few other artifacts. The house matched the description made in 1930 by Merrick. The nearby clearing covered about half an acre, where, we supposed, the potato patch and other crops must have grown. Now it was a meadow of high grasses and fireweed ringed by tall, shadowy spruces and firs that could conceal anything lurking inside them.

Skeptical as I was and accustomed to wandering alone in the deepest reaches of the Canadian wilderness, I still couldn't help but feel a bit of unease moving about this long-abandoned spot, in the shadows of ruins on the edge of a vast forest. It felt as if we were intruders in a place long since deserted, perhaps for good reason. This feeling became especially strong when the memory of those old accounts came back to me: The little girl had been playing alone in the grassy clearing one fall day when she had suddenly seen the thing come out of the woods. The description of how it had grinned at her and beckoned to her had stayed fresh in my mind, as did the note about the white mane across the top of its head. There was something in particular about those details I found unsettling. The child had fled to the house, and the creature or whatever it was had apparently then vanished into the woods. When the men, armed with guns, had later searched for it, Merrick had said they found its tracks everywhere in the surrounding area, as if it had been silently watching the family and waiting for an opportunity to appear.

That grassy clearing where the beast had been seen was the same clearing we were standing in. Only now it was much more overgrown, such that a large animal or a person could be hidden in the tall grasses without us knowing it. I found myself fidgeting with the knife in my pocket; it was hard not to imagine something sinister in the way those tall grasses swayed in the breeze, suggestive of a kind of presence—like something silently stalking through them. Beyond the clearing stood the same deep, dark woods described by Merrick, and nearby was the same house, only now it was crumbled and decayed.

I cast a glance about me at the balsam firs and spruces. "Let's explore the woods and see if we can find anything else before it gets dark," I said.

"You mean like a demon or yeti?" remarked Zach.

"I was thinking firewood," I replied.

"Oh, a demon or yeti is a bonus then," added Zach.

We cut across the clearing to the forest edge and then pushed past the branches into the shadows. The forest here was a world of vivid green sphagnum moss and a maze of grey, scaly spruces that played tricks on the eye. We searched among the spruces for any clues. These quiet, moss-draped woods felt haunted by the ghosts of Traverspine and its ultimate abandonment. Various artifacts, ranging from old wooden buckets to rusted iron tools, lay scattered about. They seemed to date from the late nineteenth through to the mid-twentieth century.

Traverspine had been founded sometime around 1840 by the Hudson's Bay Company, but the location was so isolated and remote that few trappers ever came here. Within a few years the HBC lost interest in the place. The post was taken over by a local Scottish settler who'd earlier served an apprenticeship with the HBC. This state of affairs lasted until about 1872, when the trader drifted north and the HBC again resumed control of Traverspine. But it was no more profitable and just as isolated as ever, so before long the HBC once more unloaded the post, this time to a Labrador-born trader, Joseph Michelin. Under the Michelins, the settlement at Traverspine eventually grew to three or four houses—a thriving village by Labrador standards. However, Traverspine was permanently abandoned in the years after the founding of Happy Valley-Goose Bay, when the old way of life had come to an end.

That old way of life had been filled with hardship, but also a closeness to the land and the rhythms of the natural world. The woods and waters were a part of one's life in the same way electricity and the internet are for many nowadays. Food came from fishing nets, traplines, or hunting rather than the store, supplemented by a small garden and whatever could be bartered at the trading post for the winter's supply of furs. The winters too, were long and often hungry. Every routine task took effort—chiselling ice away from the river to fetch water, chopping endless amounts of firewood, boiling water, breaking trails through deep snow, repairing snowshoes, sleds, and other vital equipment, patching the cabin's walls and roof. The most basic tool, like a pail for instance, or an axe, would be as crucial as a car or a phone is today. I picked up the decaying ruins of a wooden bucket, turning it over in my hands and trying to conjure in my mind a glimpse of this place as it was more than a century ago—it must have felt like the edge of the world.

"I think we'd better head back and make camp before dark," remarked Zach, breaking my reverie as I kneeled examining an old rusted can.

"Oh, right," I said absent-mindedly. "Good idea."

We had resolved to spend the night in the ghost settlement, pitching our tents in the shadows of the dilapidated house. The prospect was slightly nerve-racking, but we both felt it would be a shame to have come this far and not sleep here. It took some effort to haul our gear up from the riverbank, and by the time we finished, the last rays of sunlight were almost gone.

"This feels sort of like camping at Camp Crystal Lake," said Zach.

"Is that a summer camp you used to attend?" I asked.

"It's the camp from the *Friday the 13th* movies."

"Oh."

I put up my tent nearest the ruins and Zach pitched his a little closer to the woods. With the tents taken care of, we again split up. I set off to find a good place to set up our motion-activated trail camera. We wanted some means to tell if a nocturnal visitor—supernatural or otherwise—should come into our camp in the night. It turned out, however, that we'd forgotten one of the cameras in Zach's car, leaving us with only one. While I set up the lone trail camera, Zach set about gathering firewood.

I chose a spot on the edge of the clearing, strapping the camera to a sturdy balsam fir and facing it out toward the dark forest. I angled it toward where there appeared to be a slight opening in the woods, which looked like it might be an animal trail of some kind. If something did emerge from the woods in the dark, we'd hopefully have it on camera. The wind whispered through the trees as I finished lashing the camera to the tree, shivering from the cold. That done, I returned quickly to where we'd pitched our tents.

Zach had lit the fire, throwing up a flickering light that illuminated the ghostly ruins immediately behind our tents and the tall black spruces all around us, which were swaying in a slight wind. The temperature had dropped to a few degrees above freezing, and I could see my breath as I exhaled.

"This place sure is creepy at night. That house seems to almost grow in the darkness, and makes you not want to look at it," said Zach.

"The shadows seem to have that effect," I replied. "Let's boil some water and make dinner."

"Best idea I've heard all day," said Zach.

With a flashlight I dug out two freeze-dried meals and the stainless-steel cooking pot from our watertight barrel. The idea of hiking back through dark woods to the river's edge to fetch water wasn't very appealing, so instead we filled the pot with the last of our water bottles.

While we were feeding twigs and branches into the fire to make the water boil faster, we both froze instinctively at a sound in the darkness: something like a branch snapping. It had come from the woods behind our tents. I shone my flashlight in the direction of the noise. The spruces were creaking on the breeze, swaying gently with interlocked branches. There didn't seem to be anything else there.

"Probably only a red squirrel," I said.

"Yeah . . . probably," replied Zach.

Ignoring it, we turned back to the fire. When the water had boiled and our meals were cooked, we sat and ate with our backs to the darkness. The moon was rising above the silhouettes of the spruces and firs. It was, fortuitously, a full moon. By now the wind had mostly died away and the clouds had cleared, leaving the night cold and clear. The stars were brilliant, and I picked out the North Star as I sat finishing my meal. In times past, I reflected, those stars were all that humans had to guide them over the earth or the surface of the sea.

I reflected, too, on how since the dawn of time, humans have told stories of strange and scary things that lurk in the darkness, beyond the flicker of the firelight. Our earliest ancestors, huddled in caves or simple shelters, feared the sunset, when darkness descended and most large predators became active. Some of the oldest cave paintings ever found depict nameless monsters that apparently hungered for human flesh. Cultures all over the world held similar beliefs about the darkest depths of the woods, remote mountain passes, or inaccessible caves being home to flesh-eating trolls, giants, ogres, or other frightening things. Much has been made of the cultural divide between different peoples and cultures, but at least on the subject of monsters lurking in the darkness, it seems people agreed.

"We're lucky there's a full moon," I remarked, breaking the silence. "Once it rises above the treetops we should be able to see pretty well around this clearing."

Zach nodded. "These freeze-dried meals are actually pretty damn delicious," he said, finishing off his vegetable lasagna.

"Try eating them for four months straight."

"Hmm, fair enough," said Zach. "What do we do with our food at night? Put it in a tree or just move it away from the camp?"

I shook my head. "I don't bother with that normally. Sleeping on the arctic tundra with grizzlies and polar bears, there aren't any trees nearby—and usually I'm too exhausted to move my food very far. So I generally just sleep with it beside my tent."

We sat and watched the moon rise slowly above the trees, spilling its eerie silver light across the aspen saplings and fireweed and illuminating the ghostly ruins that stood beside our tents. The temperature continued to drop; it looked as if we'd have frost come morning. When the fire died, we crawled into our tents. I offered Zach the can of bear spray we'd packed. But he said he preferred his hunting knife for sleeping soundly.

7

IT COMES AT NIGHT

. . . the creature avoided the place by day but haunted it by night.
—Dr. Harry Paddon, *The Labrador Memoir of*
Dr Harry Paddon, 1912–1938

INSIDE MY TENT I arranged my gear: my extra clothing I rolled up to make a pillow, my knife and the bear spray I laid out beside me for quick access, and my little pocket flashlight I tied with some paracord to the tent's ceiling. This gave me enough light to read and make notes in my journal. I didn't feel very sleepy, though, so I figured I'd look over some of my sources about Traverspine. I pulled out Merrick's account from 1930.

Merrick had described the creature's tracks as "a strange-looking foot" that measured about twelve inches long, "narrow at the heel and forking at the front into two broad, round-ended toes." This bizarre track had been preserved in paper cut-outs, which had been laid over the tracks where they'd been found and traced. The prints, explained Merrick, were sometimes so deep that the creature "looked to weigh five hundred pounds," although at other times the "beast's mark looked no deeper than a man's track." This was very curious. The trappers and hunters who examined the prints would have been experts in the art of tracking, so simple explanations like a difference in terrain would seemingly fail to account for such a discrepancy.

The Traverspine families had set bear traps for the creature—usually a type of heavy spring trap with brutally powerful iron jaws that would clamp on an animal's leg until it could be killed. These traps were either baited with meat or else concealed under leaves along a game trail. Yet the mystery creature would apparently never go near the traps. The fear the creature occasioned spread throughout the district, and at Mud Lake, the site of a logging camp, the lumbermen even came with rifles to "lay out all night by the paths watching" for the thing, but without success.

Mud Lake was situated about eight kilometres to the northeast of Traverspine, making it the nearest inhabited place. But the nearest community with a post office was much farther—that was at Northwest River, which lay across the waters of Lake Melville, over forty kilometres away. In those days too, of course, they had no telephones or other means of communication across such lonely solitudes. The sense of isolation must have been profound. Maybe that isolation had gone to their heads at Traverspine, and caused them to hallucinate strange things?

But this wouldn't explain how dozens of eyewitnesses—most of them lumbermen or trappers from the surrounding communities—saw the strange tracks. The details in Merrick's account had also seemed to me as if they were describing real incidents. He had noted that Mrs. Michelin, the mother of the child who had been frightened by the creature's sudden appearance, had managed to get a shot off at it before it disappeared into the thick woods. The shot had apparently wounded the thing, which possibly implied it was not something supernatural after all, nor a mere figment of the imagination. Mrs. Michelin too, had noted the creature's white fur or stripe across the top of its head. For a family used to all the hardships and loneliness that life deep in the northern wilderness entailed, the Michelins were terrified enough by the incident and tracks they found to bar the door of their cabin and all sleep together, armed with guns and axes. Thereafter whenever they left their cabin, as a precaution they were always armed. For two whole winters, the creature had apparently stalked the surrounding woods. It also seemed significant that the sled dogs were frightened by it.

For a while I lay in my tent, staring at the printed page and contemplating things. On second thought, reading creepy stories alone in the dark maybe wasn't the best idea to try to get to sleep. Suddenly I thought I heard something rustling outside. I froze, straining to hear anything more. But there was only silence. At last I dismissed it as my imagination and went back to the photocopies.

The stride of the tracks, if true, was enormous. The only wild animal with a stride approaching that length would be a moose, which, when trotting or running, has a stride of about two metres. Moose also have cloven hoofs roughly like those of an ox. But a moose doesn't seem to match any other aspect of the description, and it was hard to believe that experienced trappers and hunters would fail to recognize moose tracks. To make sense of things, I decided I needed to carefully cross-examine all the accounts to see whether some clues I'd overlooked might jump out at me.

The earliest account I could find of the Traverspine crea-ture was written in 1909 by one Edward C. Robinson, a British explorer who'd come to Labrador to prospect for gold. In the Labrador interior he'd met Joseph Michelin, a local trapper, who told him the story. Like Merrick, Robinson reported that the beast had first been seen in the woods near Traverspine, and that Michelin's wife had fired at it. He also noted the same details about its having terrified the sled dogs, which were left "shivering" and "cowering"—even though these were dogs that normally wouldn't hesitate to stand and fight even the biggest bear. Robinson also reported that over a dozen men he'd met claimed to have seen the strange tracks. The tracks were "long" and had "two toes," and whatever had made them appeared to walk on only two legs. These particulars all matched Merrick's account. But Robinson's story contained some addi-tional details: he said that at night, when the creature appeared outside the houses at Traverspine, it made a "rumbling sort of whistling noise like breathing." He also wrote that on at least one occasion, there appeared to be two of them, a larger and a smaller one.

The local trappers—deeply religious and superstitious—indicated to Robinson that they thought it had been a demon, or even the Devil himself. Robinson, however, believed that what had stalked the area was some unknown survivor of the last Ice Age, when huge and terrifying creatures like sabre-tooth tigers, mastodons, and other giant animals roamed across northern Canada. Robinson hypothesized that a few surviving relics of one of these Ice Age beasts might still survive deep in the wilds of Labrador. As Robinson put it, "There is no absolute reason why they should have died out altogether . . . if there be any descendants still in existence of these prehistoric monsters, there is no more likely place to find such a creature than here."

At the same time that Robinson was exploring Labrador's wilderness, Dr. Wilfred Grenfell, the medical missionary, was travelling by ship to provide aid to isolated outposts. In the old days, life had been brutally hard in the outposts of Labrador. There had been no access to medical services; a man who was careless with an axe when chopping wood, or took a bad fall in the mountains, or met with some other accident, was likely to die a lonely death. Children died even more commonly from sickness. During harsh winters, when game was scarce and a hunter unsuccessful, famine was accepted as a fact of life. In seeking to aid the communities by providing services as a travelling doctor, Grenfell became celebrated throughout the province and beyond for his efforts. Over the years Grenfell recruited other doctors and nurses to serve in Labrador.

Knowing that he'd been active in the area near Traverspine around the same time as Merrick, I'd searched Grenfell's memoirs, published in 1919, to see whether he might have recorded anything unusual. As it turned out, he had:

Many inexplicable things happen "on Labrador." Thus, one year while visiting at the head of Hamilton Inlet, a Scotch settler came aboard to ask my advice about a large animal that had appeared round his house. Though he had sat up night after night with his gun, he had never seen it. His children had seen it several times disappearing into the trees. The French agent of Revillon Frères, twenty miles away, had come over, and together they had tracked it, measured the footmarks in the mud, and even fenced some of them round. The stride was about eight feet, the marks as of the cloven hoofs of an ox. The children described the creature as looking like a huge hairy man; and several nights the dogs had been driven growling from the house into the water. Twice the whole family had heard the creature prowling around the cottage, and tapping at the doors and windows. The now grown-up children persist in saying that they saw this wild thing. Their house is twenty miles up the large Grand River, and a hundred and fifty miles from the coast.

Dr. Grenfell stated the settler who told him the story was Scottish, but the Michelin family that lived at Traverspine was of mostly French Canadian background. So that brings up an interesting possibility—that more than one family had encountered the mysterious creature. But it's also possible that Grenfell may have simply been confused or mistaken on this point. The rest of the details are similar to Merrick's account: the children being the ones who first saw the creature among the trees, the cloven hoof tracks, the frightened dogs. Any beast that could frighten a pack of Labrador sled dogs had to be truly formidable. Labrador sled dogs were half-wolf huskies, renowned for their size and fierceness, and capable of killing a full-grown bear or even a trapper who was careless—something Grenfell mentions happened to his knowledge at least once in Labrador. Grenfell noted that the dogs would, in his words, "unhesitatingly attack even the largest polar bear."

I thought it interesting, as I lay in my tent in the dark, that Grenfell didn't dismiss the story as hoax or delusion, as a doctor might be expected to do. Instead he'd simply stated that "many inexplicable things happen 'on Labrador.'" Like Robinson, Grenfell understood the vastness of Labrador's wilderness, with its hundreds of thousands of square kilometres, and that there might easily be unaccounted things lurking deep within it.

Two of Grenfell's colleagues who'd spent years living and working in Labrador as doctors in isolated settlements near Lake Melville had also made records of the Traverspine mystery. I spread the photocopies out on my tent floor, and pen in hand, began making notes and circling key phrases in each. Most, but not all, agreed that the tracks were shaped like pointed toes or cloven hoofs. Several accounts specifically mentioned the belief that a demon or devil was haunting the woods. But some of the other chroniclers shied away from the supernatural, instead leaning more toward cryptozoology—the belief that deep in the vast, unexplored wilderness of Labrador still lived animals undocumented by modern science.

The medical doctor Harry Paddon didn't doubt the reality of the terrifying creature. Aside from intermittent visits abroad, Paddon lived in Labrador from 1912 until his death in 1939. He acted as a doctor to the trappers, lumberjacks, and fishermen along the coast, and in winter would often travel hundreds of miles by dogsled to attend to the needs of isolated settlers.

In his posthumously published memoir, Paddon recalled that, one day, the residents of Traverspine were:

> badly scared by a strange, barely human face peering at them through some willows. In alarm they rushed home and told the news. Joe being away, his wife seized a gun and, dimly seeing a figure through the bushes, fired both barrels, knowing that it was neither neighbour nor Indian. Thereafter, the creature avoided the place by day but haunted it by night. Tracks were found of which patterns were preserved. Watch was kept from places of concealment at night, but without result. The lumbermen had started work at Mud Lake at this time, and some of them joined in the hunt, but with no success. The creature evidently had a mate, as double tracks were seen, and also sounds of domestic strife were heard, with loud lamentations from the weaker member. No capture or killing was ever effected, and the affair remained a mystery. That there were gorillas or even chimpanzees in sub-arctic Labrador seems impossible. Only lately, I received from an English relation who had visited here and heard the story a newspaper cutting regarding "snowmen" whose tracks were reported by Himalayan explorers. Possibly there may be a clue here to the mystery of Traverspine, Labrador.

The details in Dr. Paddon's account overall are very similar to Merrick's and Grenfell's, with the exception that Paddon states that there was more than one of the creatures. He also differs from the others in comparing the mystery animal to a yeti (another name for which was "snowmen"), an ape-like creature rumoured to inhabit the snowy Himalayan Mountains. In any case, Paddon seemed to accept the existence of such creatures, and to think it was only a matter of time before science classified them.

That a second medical doctor with scientific training accepted the stories seemed to me significant. Paddon's colleague, Dr. C. Hogarth Forsyth, also discussed the mysterious creatures. From 1932 to 1946, Dr. Forysth operated a hospital at Cartwright, a settlement on Labrador's rugged coast about a hundred kilometres southeast of Lake Melville. Forsyth reported the tracks as being ape-like and, curiously, stated that they sometimes led to "nests under trees in the open." Forsyth explained that such prints had been "followed for as much as fifteen miles over rough country" until the trail was lost over glare ice or running water, adding that "whatever made them climbed easily over stumps and other obstructions where an ordinary man would have gone around. And whatever it was walked on two feet." Forsyth rejected any possibility that the tracks could have been made by a bear, pointing out that they were found "by trappers whose living depends on their knowledge of tracks."

"Adam?" Zach's voice suddenly came through the darkness in a hushed whisper. "Did you hear that?"

"No, wait—" I sat up in my sleeping bag. I thought I could hear a faint rustling noise on the left side of my tent, as if something had crept through the willows.

I heard Zach unzip his tent's screen door. I did the same, peering out into the moonlit clearing. There was no wind; the fireweed and high grasses were motionless, the stars above brilliant.

Zach shone his flashlight in a circle around the camp, focusing in on the thick spruce woods immediately behind his tent. "I don't see anything," he said.

"Try over by the house," I suggested.

He aimed the beam toward the crooked outline of the old house, pausing at the open window frames. It sure looked creepy in the dark. For a split second, I almost thought I caught the shape of something move inside the house. But in the darkness I couldn't be sure.

"Well, it was probably nothing," Zach said at last.

"Yeah . . . probably," I said. Zach switched off his light and rezipped his door. I hesitated for a few seconds, then went back to my notes.

I read far into the night, interrupted occasionally by the sounds of the northern wilderness. At one point, echoing from somewhere across the water, I heard the strange laughter of a loon. At intervals, too, breaking the silence of the night, came the sounds of geese landing on the river. Then, sometime well after midnight, I could distinctly hear something walking along the river, snapping branches as it went. I debated whether I should crawl out of my sleeping bag and creep off into the woods to see what it was, but I presumed it was only a bear or demon creature and ignored it.

Of the six sources I'd found regarding the Traverspine mystery, one of the most valuable was made by the New Brunswick wildlife biologist Bruce Wright, who'd visited central Labrador in 1947. Wright met with and interviewed the Michelin family who had encountered the "monster" firsthand at their Traverspine home. As a scientist, Wright was keenly interested in the mystery, and carefully recorded all that he was told:

> About 1913 the little settlement of Traverspine ... was visited in winter by two strange animals that drove the dogs to a frenzy and badly frightened the people. They left deep tracks about twelve inches long indicating great weight, and they rooted up rotten logs with great strength and they tore them apart as if searching for grubs. They sometimes stood erect on their hind legs (at which time they looked like great hairy men seven feet tall, and no doubt from this description Merrick got his title of the "Traverspine Gorilla"), but they also ran on all fours. They cleaned up some seal bones "too big for the dogs"—and what is too big for a husky is really big— and many dogs followed them and did not return ... This was a serious loss to the people as dogs were their sole means of transportation.
>
> These two strange animals, which the inhabitants called "the man" and "the woman" because one was larger than the other, stayed about the settlement despite attempts to trap them and drive them away. One day Mrs. Michelin was alone in her house with her young daughter playing at the edge of the bush behind. Suddenly the child rushed in crying, "It's following me Mummy! It's following me!" Mrs. Michelin reached for a shotgun loaded with buckshot which she always had near when her husband was away, and stepped out the back door.

"All I could see was the moving bush and the shape of a great animal standing seven feet tall in the alders. It seemed to have a sort of white ruff across the top of its head, I could not make out the rest. I fired into the bushes and I heard the shot hit. I went back into the house and bolted the door. It never came back, and there was blood where it had stood when the men from the sawmill came to look."

The sawmill operator closed down the mill and the men turned out in force to hunt, but they never found it . . . similar animals have been reported since and their tracks have been found at intervals, the latest being about 1940.

I asked Mrs. Michelin point blank if this could have been a bear. "It was no bear, Mr. Wright. I have killed twelve bears on my husband's trapline and I know their tracks well. I saw enough of this thing to be sure of that. I fired a shotgun at it and I heard the shot hit."

Huddling in my sleeping bag in the dark, the thought of some creature or creatures standing seven feet tall, driving off sled dogs, and devouring bones too big for a husky was a bit alarming. With that mental image in mind, I finally drifted off to sleep . . .

8

DOWNRIVER

The croak of the raven, the cry of the loon, and the howl of the wolf
are certainly the three characteristic sounds of the interior of Labrador.
—H. Hesketh-Prichard, *Through Trackless Labrador*, 1911

T HE SOUND OF something crashing through the bushes
woke me. Instinctively I sprang from my sleeping bag. The
first faint rays of the rising sun were streaming through the tent.
Grabbing my camera and bear spray, I unzipped the tent door,
slipped on my hiking boots, and ran toward the noise.

It was coming from the thicket by the river's edge. I paused
for a second to contemplate whether I should wake up Zach.
But I figured it was best not to disturb him. So I slowed my pace
and crept forward alone through the willows down the high
bank. My first thought was that a bear was moving about in the
thicket. Given all the tracks we'd seen, it was clear there were
many nearby.

I moved cautiously down the steep bank, one hand holding my camera, the other clutching my bear spray; the bushes
were wet from the morning dew. The sound, whatever it was,
had ceased. When I reached the water's edge I looked about.

At first I couldn't see anything—but then, on the alder-covered island in the middle of the river, I spotted the shapes of three animals. They were big, brownish things, moving half hidden among the leafy alders. Then they came into the open. Alas, it wasn't anything supernatural. Just three moose: a mother with two young calves.

I sat on the riverbank concealed in the willows and watched them. They made their way slowly across the island, the mother leading with her two calves following and grazing on the alders. When they reached the end of the island, the mother waded into the river and then swam toward the far shore. Her calves seemed to hesitate for a second at the water's edge before plunging in and swimming after her. When the moose family reached the opposite bank, they disappeared into the thick woods.

It was now about six a.m., so I headed back to our camp. Approaching our tents, the thought of sneaking up beside Zach's and scratching the door like a bear crossed my mind. But then I remembered that he slept with his knife and thought better of it. So instead I just said, "Are you still asleep?"

He mumbled a reply that I took to be confirmation he was awake.

"I just filmed three moose down by the river's edge," I said.

"You're kidding me," said Zach, apparently now wide awake.

"Yeah, it was nice—a mother and two young calves just off-shore on the island. They swam across the river. I had a great view."

"Why didn't you wake me up?"

"I didn't want to disturb you."

"The whole reason I came on this trip was to be disturbed if it meant seeing cool animals," explained Zach.

We had a quick breakfast of granola bars and green tea that we'd made the evening before and kept in our thermoses overnight. It had been a cold night, and I asked Zach how he slept. He said fine, aside from hearing a few strange noises.

After breakfast we packed up our camp. I went to retrieve the motion-activated trail camera. Inspecting the ground around it, the only tracks I found were from a moose. I couldn't see any other tracks, but the ground was hard and unlikely to register any prints of smaller animals. We wouldn't, however, be able to check the recordings until we got home, since the trail camera (a mid-range model) didn't include a screen to review images.

Our plan was to paddle back to the Churchill River and then set off down it toward the salty waters of Lake Melville. Once we reached it, we'd head east for several days until coming to one of the many wild rivers draining down from the slopes of the Mealy Mountains. These wild and ancient mountains are spread across millions of acres of wilderness, which sees few human visitors. The name "Mealy Mountains" refers to the "mealy" or powder-like patches of snow that linger on the mountains well into summer. If a Traverspine beast had ever really existed, I reasoned that it would have long since decamped from Traverspine (the area was now too close to the modern town of Happy Valley-Goose Bay) and disappeared deep into the mountain fastness. Upon this logic we'd follow one of those rivers into the heart of the mountains, and then continue on foot to explore the surrounding caves for anything unusual. That was the plan anyway.

Zach agreed with it wholeheartedly, even the bits about canoeing along the windy expanse of Lake Melville and battling upriver into the mountains (which I'd warned him would be brutally difficult). He was proving to be an excellent expedition partner.

Although it was now well into September, once the sun had climbed above the horizon things warmed up quite a bit, and the wind died enough that clouds of mosquitoes and even blackflies soon materialized. They attacked our faces, behind our ears, and our necks. Fortunately, once we'd made it back to the swifter current of the Churchill River, our pace in the canoe was fast enough to leave most of the bugs behind. We kept to the river's southern shore, passing wooded, sandy banks that in many places had been eroded by the strong current. Sometimes this erosion caused landslides where whole sections of the bank tumbled into the river, taking trees with them. It was a reminder not to pitch one's tent too close to the river's edge.

Seeing how it was actually my first time canoeing with a former dairy farmer turned mixed martial arts fighter, I took the opportunity to learn as much as I could about cows and fighting. From my seat in the stern, as we paddled along, I quizzed Zach about these subjects, which had hitherto never been very high on my list of research interests.

"Aren't you at all worried about suffering brain damage from all these fights?" I asked cheerfully as we paddled to the peaceful sounds of warblers and other songbirds along the banks. The day had blossomed into a fine September morning.

"Well, no, not overly anyway," Zach replied from the bow with an air of thoughtfulness. "I think if you're smart you can avoid that, and I don't intend to keep doing MMA fights forever. Eventually I'll retire."

"That's sounds sensible," I said, drawing a stroke of my paddle. "So in MMA you're allowed to punch and kick people in the face?"

"Yes, you can do pretty much anything, except low blows and eye gouges," replied Zach.

"And if you win a fight, how much money do you generally get?" Just then a hooded merganser, a handsome type of duck, skidded down across the river to the left of us.

"It depends on the ticket sales, but in the league I mostly fight in, it's about a thousand dollars or so for a win."

"That's not bad," I said. "And if you lose?"

"About half that."

"And that's why you do it? For the money?" I asked.

"No." Zach stared out across the water. "I do it because there's no better feeling in the world than the thrill of landing the perfect punch or kick in your opponent's face and seeing him go down like a sack of bricks."

Our progress downriver was quite rapid; given the strong current, we were able to maintain a swift paddling pace with relative ease. The river was exceptionally wide, nearly three kilometres across. Fortunately, there was little wind. In places its span was broken up by large forested islands, where beavers cut aspens and shorebirds hopped along looking for insects.

Zach had grown up on a two-hundred-acre farm. He attributed the hard farm chores of his upbringing (the cows had to be milked twice a day) to his early success in fights. I recalled stories from our school days of cow-tipping exploits.

"Never happened," Zach asserted. "Cow tipping is just a myth."

"You're kidding me?"

"No, literally impossible. You can't tip a cow."

I stopped paddling. "But what if a bunch of people all rushed the cow at once?"

"Nope, can't be done," said Zach confidently. "First, cows don't sleep standing up. That's a myth. Two, they're heavy and strong, and wouldn't just tip over if you pushed one. The cow would move out of the way before it tipped."

"So there's no way it could be done?"

"I don't see any practical way it could be done. At least, not by a group of people sneaking into a cow pasture at night and running at a cow."

"What about all the stories of cow tipping?"

"Just myths made up," Zach said again. "Look it up on YouTube if you don't believe me—you won't find a single video anywhere of someone actually succeeding in tipping a cow."

I nodded. Our trip was proving to be very educational so far.

—

By the time we reached Lake Melville the skies had clouded over and rain threatened. It was a reminder that weather could change quickly along these northern coasts. Still we pressed on, paddling through a labyrinth of willow- and alder-covered islands. The island maze helped shelter us from the vast open waters of Lake Melville, which I knew could be quite stormy and dangerous to paddle on in a small canoe. The lake, actually a giant bay, extends about a hundred and seventy kilometres inland from the North Atlantic, and at its widest point it's nearly forty kilometres across. Seals, whales, and even the odd Greenland shark lurk in its murky waters. In rough weather, Melville's waves are easily large enough to swamp a canoe.

Near the entrance to the lake the water was still fresh, or mostly fresh, and as yet we couldn't smell the sea air. The screeching cry of ospreys hunting overhead punctuated the air, while along the weedy shorelines swam green-winged teals as well as large flocks of Canada geese, more mergansers, and seagulls. Meanwhile, in the shallows, sandpipers and greater yellowlegs waded along, hunting for invertebrates. Soon all these birds would be headed south for warmer climes.

Labrador's wild shores had also once been home to the great auk, a large flightless bird with black and white feathers resembling a sort of penguin. Unfortunately for the great auks, their inability to fly made them an easy meal for early explorers. Jacques Cartier had his crews capture the birds as food rations for their stormy voyage home across the ocean. The auk's huge eggs were also an attractive food source for half-famished sailors, and its soft feathers were highly valued for use in pillows. By the 1700s the birds were becoming endangered and were the focus of some of the earliest conservation laws. In 1775, Newfoundland's colonial authorities actually banned hunting great auks or collecting their eggs (offenders caught poaching the birds were publicly whipped), though it was still permitted to use the auks for fishing bait. But despite these measures the number of great auks continued to dwindle, and by the 1850s they were extinct.

Nor was the great auk the only Labrador bird to suffer such a fate. Labrador's rugged coastline had also once been home to the Labrador duck, a type of sea duck that fed on clams and mussels. Unlike the great auks, the Labrador duck had always been rare and elusive; ornithologists believe that its population was never large. The last of these ducks were seen in the 1870s, before they too vanished.

I drew my paddle through the water, daydreaming about ducks and great auks, half wondering whether, hidden away in some wild corner of Labrador, a few might yet survive. Of course, I knew this wasn't possible, but I liked the thought of it just the same.

As we pushed on, a drizzling rain began to fall. This soon increased to a steady downpour, which began to fill up the canoe. Still, the winds were light, so we kept paddling to take advantage of the calm conditions. In the heavy rain, however, it was difficult to see much beyond the shoreline. We couldn't make out the far side of the bay, and even the surrounding mountains were completely concealed by thick rain clouds. Eventually we passed beyond the islands and came out into the open expanse of Lake Melville. Paddling on such a vast body of water, especially in September, might have a been a little unnerving in so small a vessel, but as it was, the heavy rain made it hard to tell just how big a water body it really was. In any case, we kept as close to shore as we could.

The long hours paddling gave us plenty of time to discuss the Traverspine beast and the reading I'd done in my tent. We both agreed that a hoax was entirely unlikely. In the first case, in such an isolated place as Traverspine, it wasn't as if one could simply pop over to the local costume shop and order up a gorilla suit. In the second, with virtually everyone in Labrador from childhood on armed with a rifle or shotgun and well able to use it, the notion of wandering about the woods after dark in a costume to prank a neighbour would seem reckless in the extreme. Indeed, the accounts agreed that Mrs. Michelin had gotten off a shot at the beast, whatever it was. The sightings and encounters had also continued through several winters, and it seemed unlikely that anyone would keep up a hoax that long and across such a remote area. Furthermore, there were the tracks—it would be hard to fake them enough to fool seasoned trappers. But even if we were prepared to somehow overlook all these objections, there was no discounting the fear displayed by dozens of tough, half-wolf sled dogs—no keen-nosed husky that had faced wolves or bears would fail to distinguish the human scent beneath a costume or cower in fear from a mere human prankster. As Dr. Grenfell had noted, the huskies wouldn't hesitate to attack even a polar bear. And yet whatever had appeared at Traverspine had scared them stiff and even driven them into the river.

I speculated that a shipwreck returning from tropical climes might have stranded a chimpanzee or gorilla. A male gorilla stands nearly six feet tall, weighs up to five hundred pounds, and has incredible strength and impressive canines. However, I could find nothing in any historical sources or archives to suggest that any such shipwreck had ever occurred on the Labrador coast. More to the point, this theory foundered on the rocks when it occurred to me that any escaped chimpanzee or gorilla wouldn't have a chance of surviving even a week in the bitterly cold winter, when temperatures dropped to forty below. The accounts seemed clear on the point that the creature(s) had stalked the area around Traverspine for at least two winters, which definitely ruled out this theory.

"What do you make of it all?" I asked Zach as I drew a j-stroke of my paddle. The heavy downpour had finally lightened back to a mere drizzle. We were somewhere along the coast of Lake Melville, the shoreline half hidden in drifting mist.

"I don't know. I'm a lot less confident in my mangy polar bear theory than I was before we came here." Zach sat gazing at the mist-shrouded spruce forests from the canoe's bow. "I'm sure of one thing though."

"What's that?" I asked.

"I'm glad I bought a bigger knife for this trip."

9

INTO THE FOG

Where death's cold and shrouded mantle lurks in fogs from Labrador,
And the demons of destruction haunt a wild and dangerous shore
—William Lawrence Chittenden,
"Captain John 'Atlantic' Brown," 1894

P ADDLING THROUGH FOG AND RAIN, our strokes unin-
terrupted for hours on end, almost lulled us into a sort of
trance—a feeling accentuated by our wild surroundings. When
the rain finally lifted we could see misty mountains in the distance across the water, their summits concealed in thick clouds.
That wasn't all: far off shore loomed a strange-looking object.
At first we thought it might be a small island, but as our paddle strokes brought us closer, we realized it was actually a ship
that had run aground. It looked like an old iron-hulled fishing
schooner, about thirty-five feet long and with two masts and a
small cabin. The hull was badly rusted, and the vessel listed to
the starboard side; water had flooded below decks. It must have
been stranded on the rocks for decades at least. It was a somewhat eerie sight, a ghost ship abandoned far from shore.

I'd read of sailors shipwrecked or marooned along Labrador's rugged coastline, an occurrence that generally didn't end well. In 1861, for example, some American whalers deserted their ship and headed for the bleak Labrador shore. Given the icy seas, foggy coastline, and lack of food and fresh water, things didn't go all that smoothly. Of the nine sailors on board, three were murdered and eaten by the others. The rest eventually made it to Nain, a tiny coastal settlement in northern Labrador, where I like to think they lived happily ever after.

The Vikings, too, had sailed these waters over a thousand years ago. Once, according to the ancient sagas, a large party of Vikings overwintered on the Labrador coast. The winter proved a harsh one with storms that whipped the sea into a fury, preventing the Vikings from venturing out in their boats to fish. Hunting also failed to provide enough food for the entire party, which numbered around a hundred and sixty people. Tensions rose as their plight worsened, with divisions breaking out among those who worshipped the old gods and those who followed the new religion, Christianity. Then one day, in the pounding surf along the coast, a whale washed up. While some might guess that the Vikings rushed out to try to save it by pushing it into deeper water, instead the Vikings joyously hacked it up with their broad swords. They then boiled up its blubber and meat for a great feast.

The whale, reportedly, was of a strange type that no one recognized—not even their leader, an Icelander named Karlsefni, who was an experienced whale hunter. Regardless, they happily ate it. But in the midst of the feast a dispute arose when one member of the party, an old wanderer named Thorhall, proclaimed that the beached whale had been a gift from Thor. Thorhall, it turned out, had gone off on his own and prayed to Thor to deliver them. This revelation offended the recently converted Christians among the Vikings, who thereafter refused to eat any more whale meat. When the Labrador winter at last ended, the Vikings split up; those who still worshipped the old gods elected to follow Thorhall north along the desolate Labrador coast, while the rest followed Karlsefni south. But luck wasn't with Thorhall and his men. After sailing north they tried to head westward back to Greenland, only, in the words of the saga, to run "into fierce headwinds that drove them right across to Ireland. There they were brutally beaten and enslaved; and there Thorhall died."

After canoeing nearly fifty kilometres, Zach and I at last made camp on a sandy beach framed by dark woods. The beach was part of the lee side of a big peninsula jutting into the bay. The effects of the tide were now clearly visible, so we made sure to put our tents well above the high-water line. We were getting closer to the open ocean, and also closer to the haunts of polar bears. Behind our tents were dune grasses and what looked like a kind of wild wheat—which reminded me of the Vikings' voyages to Labrador and their ancient sagas' account of finding "self-sown" wheat when they landed. Inspecting the woods, I noted that there were white spruce as well as black spruce, some birch, balsam firs, and even a few mountain ashes.

There was also plenty of driftwood washed up along the shore, allowing us to make a blazing fire with which to boil water and cook supper. The wind had picked up considerably, blowing stiff and cold from the west. Our life jackets and clothing, soaked by the heavy downpour earlier, we strung up on a make-shift clothesline. My insulated rain jacket had once been able to keep me bone-dry in even the heaviest rain, but tattered and torn after years of adventures, it no longer kept the wetness out as well as it once did.

With the temperature dropping, we were glad of the fire. As we sat finishing our freeze-dried meals on a big driftwood log that had washed ashore, we were treated to a hauntingly surreal sunset. Above us the skies had cleared, but far across the bay's windy expanse, thick clouds still lingered above the dark mountains. The silhouetted mountains concealed the sun's orb, but it illuminated the sky and clouds above them with a brilliant red glow. The whole scene seemed like a strange dream, an effect that felt all the stronger given the ghost ship we'd seen earlier. Stranger still to think, as I did, that those same enchanting mountains across the water had once borne silent witness to Viking ships under sail here and birch bark canoes. For a moment it was almost as if we had a glimpse through a portal to another, vanished world.

Sitting on the windswept and lonely beach, with the darkening sky above us and the deep woods behind, I remembered some of the stories I'd come across in the oral history accounts I'd been reading. Ever since the Viking voyages more than a thousand years ago, tales had been told of the strange things found in Labrador. In addition to the one-legged uniped that had killed Thorvald, the ancient sagas spoke of phantoms along these fog-bound, rocky shores. Indeed, for a land as sparsely inhabited as Labrador, ghost-haunted valleys and nightly apparitions seemed to be everywhere.

One story came from an old trapper, who recounted how he'd gone hunting for partridges near a remote cove along the Labrador coast, on the far side of the Mealy Mountains from where we were camped. Near the cove stood a small hill, which was reputed to be haunted by the ghost of a half-crazed trapper who'd died nearby. The ghost, it was said, wouldn't tolerate any intrusion, and would knock over the tea kettle of any trapper or hunter who stopped on the hill to make a fire. But the trapper on this occasion ignored the story and climbed the hill regardless to make a fire and boil a pot of water. It was a calm day, but to his bewilderment, no matter what he tried, his pot of water wouldn't stay upright over the fire—again and again it mysteriously tipped over, spilling out its contents and extinguishing the fire. The angry ghost wouldn't put up with anyone disturbing its campsite—and so the stubborn trapper, learning his lesson, soon packed up his supplies and never again stopped at the haunted hill. Just then our pot fell over, spilling its contents into our fire and half extinguishing it.

"Damn wind," said Zach as he rose from his seat on the driftwood log to refill the kettle.

"Yeah . . . wind," I said, looking around suspiciously at the surroundings bushes.

When we'd finished our tea, warmed ourselves sufficiently, and dried our wet clothes, we said goodnight and crawled into our tents.

—

It was a wild and windy night; in the early morning I awoke to the sounds of my tent shaking violently in the strong winds and the ominous cries of a raven somewhere nearby. It seemed a miracle that our tents hadn't blown down in the night. Fortunately, we'd taken the precaution of piling rocks on top of our tent pegs, which we'd buried in the sand. Crawling out of my tent, I saw whitecaps riddling the bay we'd crossed, but the skies were mostly clear, revealing an encircling wall of blue mountains, which the day before we'd only partially seen given the clouds. There didn't appear to be any signs of life from Zach's tent, so I wandered off down the beach to look for something to eat.

So far, everywhere we stopped a variety of wild berries were easily found, and here was no exception. On the edge of the spruce woods were plenty of delicious wild currants. I ate a bunch of these, but with the winds chilling my hands, I soon moved off the beach and into the shelter of the woods. In the forest were some tart lingonberries and juicy crowberries, which I happily added to my breakfast.

As the sun crept above the horizon the wind seemed only to grow stronger. This alarmed me a little: we still had miles of open water to traverse before reaching the mouth of the mountain river we were seeking. With the gusts this strong, canoeing would be a challenge. I decided it was best to go and see if Zach was awake, and that we should be on our way without delay, before the wind got any worse.

When I reached camp, I found Zach already awake and kneeling beside his tent, examining something in the sand.

"What is it?" I asked, coming up beside him.

"Tracks."

"What kind?"

"Not sure."

I bent down and inspected the prints. I could barely believe it—*they were lynx tracks*. Each print was made up of four roughly circular marks sunk into the sand, which could only be the tracks of some type of wild cat. The telltale sign was the absence of claw marks: fox and wolf tracks always have them, whereas cats have retractable claws, which don't show up in their prints. And since there weren't any bobcats or mountain lions around here, that meant these had to be lynx tracks. Plus, the tracks were large, which was further indicative of a lynx: they have giant, oversized paws that act as snowshoes, allowing them to walk over deep snow. It was a thrill to think a lynx—an animal so elusive it seems almost semi-mythical, like a grey phantom of the north woods—had stalked right past our tents in the night. But there wasn't any time to gawk at the tracks or try to follow them. The wind was rising, and we had to take advantage of whatever morning calm remained to get off this peninsula. With the season already advanced, time wasn't on our side.

"Let's get going before this wind gets any worse," I said.

"How far to the river's mouth?" asked Zach, eyeing the whitecaps that riddled the wide-open expanse of water we had to cross.

"About ten kilometres," I replied.

"Looks like a pretty rough crossing," said Zach.

We strapped on our waterproof waders, loaded up the canoe, and heaved it down to the waterline. It was now low tide, which promised to make our task even more difficult—we'd have to canoe far off shore, at least half a kilometre out, to find water deep enough to paddle. Along Lake Melville, at least what we'd seen of it, are extensive shallows filled with boulders. It was one such stretch of shallows that had proved the undoing of the marooned ship we'd seen the day before.

With Zach in the bow and me in the stern, we paddled with everything we had, battling a strong easterly wind that constantly threatened to drive us into the shallows. The sea was muddy and churned up all around us. Despite the danger of getting swamped by the waves, it was actually easier to paddle farther offshore in the deeper water than it was to battle the breaking surf in the shallows. We pushed on, driving hard across the bay to a small gap in the green trees on the far shore. This marked the opening of a large inner bay—and somewhere in there, according to our maps, we'd find the river that would lead us into the mountains.

Suddenly, with a thud, a big wave hit our canoe broadside, splashing water over the gunwales. Fortunately, though, it'd take more than one splash to sink us. I adjusted my steering to angle the canoe offshore into the waves. This meant taking a less direct route across and therefore more strenuous paddling to get where we needed to go, but by angling into each big wave we'd be less likely to swamp, which seemed prudent. Resting, even for a moment, was impossible; we were far from shore now and needed all our strength just to keep the canoe plowing forward across the choppy water.

Even so, we couldn't prevent more waves from spilling over the canoe. The water began to accumulate, swishing and slosh-ing around our knees and drenching our backpacks, which lay stowed in the canoe. I'd been in some tight scrapes paddling on big bodies of water before—once near the mouth of the Harricana River on James Bay, another time in the High Arctic on Victoria Island, and during my solo crossing of Canada's mainland Arctic—but these stiff September winds off the Labrador coast were proving quite the challenge.

"Should we be at all alarmed by these waves?" shouted Zach from the bow.

"It'll take more than this to sink us!" I shouted back. Confidence, I figured, was half the battle.

"Right, on we go then." Zach swung another stroke of his paddle into an oncoming wave. I knew from past experience that the canoe could hold a lot of water before actually sinking, and fortunately we were still nowhere near that point. If we could just reach the narrow gap that led to the inner bay, we'd be able to escape the open lake and regroup on the bay's sheltered side.

Hard paddling drove us onward, zigzagging our way into the waves to avoid capsizing, while trying to reach the sheltered gap. As an added hazard, concealed in the muddy, turbulent waters were big boulders, which it wouldn't be wise to slam into. Mostly we could spot these boulders by the furious breaking surf around them, but there were some less exposed ones that didn't give themselves away so easily. These were the real hazards; we had to keep a sharp eye out to avoid smashing into them.

At last we reached the safety of the narrow gap, avoiding the full force of the wind sweeping across miles of open water, and now tucking into the lee side of a wooded shoreline. It was a big, beautiful bay we'd come into, with wonderful sandy shorelines and enchanting-looking woods of spruce and fir. Clustered around the near shore we could make out ten or so small cabins or cottages—these, we knew, belonged to people in Happy Valley-Goose Bay. Most, however, looked deserted now, with only a few motorboats anchored outside them.

Across the bay we had for the first time a good view of the Mealy Mountains, the ancient weathered peaks that look down upon Lake Melville's southern shore. They looked majestic and mysterious, their windswept summits hidden in misty clouds, and their lower slopes cloaked in dark conifer forests. It was those wild mountains that we were headed into.

10

LEGENDS OF LONG AGO

There lieth a wreck on the dismal shore
Of cold and pitiless Labrador
— Thomas Moore, "Passing Deadman's Island," 1804

T HE LITTLE-KNOWN WATERWAY we were seeking, labelled on our maps as the Kenemich River, flows out of the Mealy Mountains. Our plan was to follow it upstream into the mountains, using whatever means necessary to overcome its swift current: paddling, poling off the bottom, wading, hauling with ropes. As the crow flies, the mountains were approximately twenty kilometres inland—but in practice, with all the river's winding bends, the true distance we'd have to cover would be far greater. For at least some of that distance, I knew we'd have to travel on foot, as there could be little doubt that eventually the river's raging torrent would become too strong to navigate. The land itself, which lay between the mountain ranges and the sea, was an almost impassable barrier of trackless muskeg, deadfall, thick woods, and steep forested hills.

It wasn't going to be easy: an earlier explorer, J.M. Scott, back in 1928 had the same idea of following the Kenemich River to explore the Mealy Mountains. Scott was part of a British-led mapping expedition to central Labrador, but for the Kenemich, he split from the main party to tackle it alone. Scott never reached the mountains, giving up after three days of misery. To quote his words:

> The river meandered aimlessly and its banks were of such soft mud that it was impossible to walk along them. I was forced into the woods, where I tore my clothes on the branches, and since I could rarely see more than fifty yards ahead I failed to keep an accurate compass traverse ... It seemed that my only chance of being useful was to reach the Mealy Mountains and get a comprehensive view from one of the barren peaks. I had no tent and, to increase my speed, I had dumped my sleeping-bag. It rained and I spent two uncomfortable nights. At last I climbed a tree and saw some fifteen miles of the same dismal country between me and the bare mountain slopes. I climbed down and walked back to Carter Basin a wiser but a worse dressed man ...

Hopefully, we'd meet with more success than Scott did.

Our escape from the fierce winds proved only fleeting, however. To reach the Kenemich River's mouth, we soon had to leave the sheltered point and strike across the inner bay, labelled on our map as Carter Basin, which was over five kilometres wide. The wind here was as fierce as ever, and it was a battle with all our strength to make headway. Luckily, though, the waves weren't quite as large as they'd been earlier on the wide-open expanse of Lake Melville.

Eventually we crossed the bay, coming upon wild shores with tall grasses and lots of driftwood. An Arctic tern—a graceful shorebird with a black-capped head—soared along the coastline hunting for fish. When it spotted one, it hovered like a helicopter, then dove with tremendous speed into the water, spearing the fish with its sharp beak. Along with hummingbirds, they're among the few bird species in the world that have that ability to hover. Ever since I'd first seen an Arctic tern soaring on the coast of Hudson Bay, I'd counted them as one of my favourite birds.

The river's mouth we found hidden behind a spruce-covered island and a long, willow-covered point. There were also some mud flats with a great quantity of driftwood washed ashore. The sight of all this driftwood—mostly full-sized dead spruce trees—made me a little uneasy. The trees had evidently been carried downstream from the river, which seemed to bode ill for what we might find on our arduous journey upstream—in all probability, impenetrable logjams that would necessitate gruelling portages. I'd spent much of the summer already dealing with logjams on isolated rivers, and there are few things more difficult than struggling around logjams with heavy loads while being eaten alive by blackflies and mosquitoes. But that was alone, and now I had Zach, so looking on the bright side, things might prove easier. At least I hoped so.

Near the river's mouth were sandy shallows, which we couldn't paddle across, especially with the fierce winds. So instead we jumped overboard, and in our waders simply towed the canoe behind us as we staggered against the wind toward deeper water. We were both feeling pretty badly dehydrated. We

"The road was but a tiny, narrow ribbon in the midst of a sea of sombre spruce and tamaracks, which even today undoubtedly hid places no human foot had ever trod."

"We didn't drive thirty-two hours to turn back now." Zach strapping on his waterproof waders on the banks of the Churchill River.

Paddling up the Traverspine River.

Zach and I unpacking the gear and climbing the steep bank into the woods.

Zach searching the labyrinthine woods for any hint of ruins.

"Ahead, on the edge of the forest, loomed the crumbling ruins of a two-storey wood house."

The mother moose leading her two young calves across the island.

Paddling down the Churchill River toward Lake Melville.

"At first we thought it might be a small island, but as our paddle strokes brought us closer, we realized it was actually a ship that had run aground."

" . . . far across the bay's windy expanse, thick clouds still lingered above the dark mountains. The silhouetted mountains concealed the sun's orb, but it illuminated the sky and clouds above them with a brilliant red glow. The whole scene seemed like a strange dream, an effect that felt all the stronger given the ghost ship we'd seen earlier."

"I bent down and inspected the prints. I could barely believe it—*they were lynx tracks.*"

"Perched in the tallest spruces were often nesting ospreys, their harsh, raspy cries ringing out like a challenge whenever we passed below in the canoe..."

A trio of curious river otters in the Kenemich River.

Zach dragging the canoe up the Kenemich River.

"Taking turns controlling the canoe, we moved elf-like along the rocks, jumping from slippery boulder to slippery boulder."

hadn't had a chance to replenish our water bottles since leaving Traverspine, as we found Lake Melville too salty to drink, unless one was really desperate.

Zach bent down and sampled some of the water near the river's mouth. "Still a little salty," he reported.

We pushed on without filling our bottles. After a few more minutes of wading, the river became deep enough for us to switch back to paddling. Finally, when we came across an alder-covered island a few hundred metres up the river, we figured we were far enough inland that the water would no longer be salty. We landed the canoe on the island and went ashore to refill our bottles. The river was muddy from all the sediments washed into it along its banks, but we had my hand-held carbon-filter purifier, and so we pumped the river water through it to refill our bottles.

While Zach was busy pumping water, I wandered down the island's shore. I thought I could hear a distant drone, like a boat engine. But it might only have been the wind roaring far away across the bay. I paused and listened; the sound grew steadily louder. There was no mistaking it: it was an engine all right.

A few minutes later, from the direction of the bay, a flat-bottomed aluminum boat appeared. At the motor was an older man, dressed in hunting camouflage, while standing in front of him was a Labrador retriever. He'd probably spotted us crossing the bay, an unusual sight no doubt, and had followed us here. But surprisingly he passed us in the motorboat, gunning the engine hard in order to overcome the river's swift current.

"I wonder where he's headed," said Zach.

"I don't imagine he can get very far in a motorboat," I replied. "Given the topography, there must be rapids not too far upstream."

Zach resumed his pumping to fill up his water bottle. Then, only a few minutes later, while we were still standing on the island, we heard the roar of the engine again. The man had piloted his boat around and come back downstream.

This time he slowed his engine and coasted in toward the muddy shoreline. Beside him in the boat lay a shotgun. I waved. The man nodded while the boat drifted into the soft mud and the dog jumped out eagerly.

"Hello," Zach said.

The man nodded sheepishly. "Where did you come from?"

"Happy Valley," I said.

"You came all the way here in that little canoe?"

"Yes," I said, petting the dog. I think the man expected some further explanation on our part. I was about to say we were off to find a demon monster, but somehow the right words didn't come, and in the end I said nothing further. Zach also seemed reluctant to divulge our exact plans.

"Where you heading?" the man in the boat asked.

"Upriver," I said vaguely.

He nodded slowly, but from his look, he seemed perplexed at the idea. No doubt the notion of canoeing against the current of a mountain river seemed a strange plan.

"But how you gonna get upriver?" he continued.

"With that canoe," said Zach, pointing at it.

"Oh." He nodded slowly, looking at us doubtfully.

"Are you duck hunting?" I asked.

He nodded again, without elaborating. Then a moment later, apparently having made up his mind about us, he abruptly called to his dog, which jumped back into the boat. With a wave at us, he revved the engine. "Good luck!" he shouted before disappearing back downriver.

"Hmm, that was strange," I said, "how he was supposedly hunting but only went up and back in a few minutes. If you were hunting ducks, you'd think you'd want to sit quietly and wait for a bit."

"I think he was just curious about what these two idiots were doing in a canoe," said Zach.

—

As we paddled hard upriver, high, steep banks and thick encircling woods completely hid the mountains from view. The lower slopes were a tangled mass of impenetrable alders ten feet high, while higher up the slopes grew black and white spruces, balsam firs, birch, and poplars. Perched in the tallest spruces were often nesting ospreys, their harsh, raspy cries ringing out like a challenge whenever we passed below in the canoe, paddling steadily against the swift current.

In my tent I'd been continuing to study the sources and ponder the evidence. One possible explanation for the Traverspine mystery had been suggested by Professor Wright, the wildlife biologist who'd travelled to Labrador in the 1940s and interviewed Mrs. Michelin. Wright had wondered if what had terrorized the Michelin family might not have been a barrenland grizzly bear. Grizzlies are common in Canada's western Arctic—on my 2017 solo journey I'd come across over a dozen of them—but they range only as far east as Hudson Bay. As the bird flies, that's well over two thousand kilometres west of

Traverspine. These barren-land grizzlies, also known as arctic grizzlies, roam across the tundra devouring caribou and muskox as well as wild berries, roots, willow shoots, salmon, and other fish. They're an impressive animal, as I could testify from having met them outside my tent at night. But could a grizzly have ended up in Labrador?

There are in fact old legends and alleged sightings of grizzlies in Labrador, as well as on neighbouring Quebec's Ungava Peninsula, but in the absence of hard proof, scientists were long skeptical of these claims. From my doctoral research on Indigenous legends, I knew that the Naskapi (Innu) had a tradition about a "great bear" called *mishta-utshekatak^u* or *mɪstuːtʃeːkətaːkʷ*, which was said to be much larger than a black bear, with very long claws, and very dangerous. Most anthropologists, however, believe that this "great bear" was only a myth. But I wasn't so sure.

In 1906, in his book *The Long Labrador Trail*, American explorer Dillon Wallace related an intriguing story he'd heard while exploring Labrador a few years earlier:

> There is a story of a very large and ferocious brown bear that tradition says inhabits the barrens to the eastward toward George River. Mr. Peter McKenzie told me that many years ago, when he was stationed at Fort Chimo, the Indians brought him one of the skins of this animal, and Ford [another fur trader] at George River said that, some twenty years since, he saw a piece of one of the skins. Both agreed that the hair was very long, light brown in colour, silver tipped and of a decidedly different species from either the polar or

black bear. This is the only definite information as to it that I was able to gather. The Indians speak of it with dread, and insist that it is still to be found, though none of them can say positively that he has seen one in a decade. I am inclined to believe that the brown bear, so far as Labrador is concerned, has been exterminated.

The surveyor Albert Peter Low, whose records had proven useful so far, also had something to say on the subject of grizzlies in Labrador. Writing of his experiences exploring the region in 1894, Low said he had "no doubt" that grizzlies lived in Labrador, noting that "skins are brought in at intervals to Fort Chimo, and the Nascaupee Indians have numerous tales of its size and ferocity."

Similar circumstantial reports of grizzlies convinced Professor Wright that the bears really had once roamed Labrador, and had only recently gone extinct. Wright concluded that what had haunted Traverspine for several winters was none other than one of these last surviving grizzlies. He argued that, despite Mrs. Michelin's and the others' insistence that it was no bear, she and the other locals had only ever encountered black bears, and therefore weren't familiar with grizzlies and wouldn't have recognized the Traverspine creatures as such. Grizzly bears are not only much larger than black bears and have different coloured fur, they have much broader shoulders, with a distinctive shoulder hump, and a wider, almost angular face. They also have much longer, curved claws.

At first Wright's theory seemed a bit of a stretch to me. But I was aware that a significant archaeological discovery had occurred since Wright's death, one that partly supported his conjecture. In 1975, the archaeologist Dr. Steven Cox, while excavating an Inuit site in northern Labrador, found a well-preserved bear skull dating to the eighteenth century. Analysis of the teeth confirmed that it was neither a black bear nor a polar bear: *it was a grizzly.* This finally proved beyond doubt that grizzly bears really had once lived in Labrador, just as legend had long maintained and as Wright had believed. So that aspect of Wright's theory was at least correct. But there were still some obvious stumbling blocks to jumping to the conclusion that this is what had terrified Traverspine. For one thing, although there seemed to be agreement that Labrador grizzlies had been ferocious and terrifying, in almost all other respects a grizzly didn't match the eyewitness descriptions from Traverspine. It was all very curious.

In my tent at night, reading over by flashlight one of the earliest records I'd photocopied—an old fur trader's journal from more than two hundred years ago—I suddenly sat up in disbelief. The account I'd been studying, *A Journal of Transactions and Events, During a Residence of Nearly Sixteen Years on the Coast of Labrador*, had been published in 1792 by George Cartwright, one of the first English settlers in Labrador. Cartwright's journal was full of interesting observations, but the passage that really caught my attention was in the middle of a discussion of different kinds of wildlife:

> The beasts ... [include] bears both white and black (of the
> latter I am told, there are two kinds, one of which have a
> white ring round their necks, and the Esquimaux [Inuit] say,

"They are very ferocious," but I never saw one of them or even
a skin) . . .

This passage about a mysterious kind of bear that had a "white ring round their necks" immediately made me think of the accounts of the Traverspine beast having a "white ruff" across the top of its head. From my experiences in western Canada I knew that grizzlies often have a silverish-white colour on their neck or backs, but to read Cartwright's description of a ferocious bear with a "white ring" seemed too great a coincidence to overlook. That did sound strikingly similar to the eye-witness reports of the scary creature at Traverspine's "white ruff."

Had Professor Wright been on to something after all? For a long while I sat and pondered the evidence, unsure whether to agree or disagree with Wright. There could be no doubt that a grizzly bear might "clean up seal bones too big for a dog," and that it might also have frightened the children and driven off or even killed (and eaten) huskies. But at the same time, a grizzly didn't seem to match any other aspect of the descriptions. Wright said he'd asked Mrs. Michelin "point blank if this could have been a bear," and that she'd insisted: *It was no bear Mr. Wright. I have killed twelve bears on my husband's trapline and I know their tracks well. I saw enough of this thing to be sure of that.* Dr. Forsyth had also stated that the creature was certainly no bear. And a grizzly bear's tracks aren't that different from a black bear's. The question seemed to hinge on whether it was really the case, as Professor Wright assumed, that the local Labrador settlers would have failed to recognize a grizzly.

As it turned out, there was evidence to suggest Wright was wrong about that, and that the local settlers knew about grizzlies, or at least rumours about them. The naturalist Farley Mowat, who wasn't writing about Traverspine but nevertheless was interested in grizzlies, noted in 1984 that his friend Harold Horwood, the Newfoundland writer and naturalist, had told him that "Labrador natives, both white and Indian, state positively that the [grizzly] bears were once found as far to the south and east as the Mealy Mountains, a barren, broken range between Goose Bay and Cartwright." Horwood's statement is significant not only because it specifically mentions the Mealy Mountains as a place where grizzlies once lived, but also because it matches reports like Albert Peter Low's, which had similarly suggested that grizzlies weren't unknown. This then is hard to reconcile with Wright's assumption that the local Labradorians knew nothing about grizzlies. This led me to think that Wright's theory had to be mistaken, but what proved to be the final nail in the coffin for it was that Wright's own research contradicted it.

Wright heard that in 1928, John Michelin, who lived in Northwest River, had seen a grizzly at close range while guiding two American hunters in northern Labrador, and that another Michelin had even once shot and killed a grizzly near Goose Bay. Wright saw this as evidence that grizzlies existed in Labrador, but curiously didn't see how it would also suggest that the Michelins—and other local trappers of the day—wouldn't have failed to make the connection between the Traverspine beast and grizzlies if that's what it had really been. In short, Wright's grizzly theory rested on two premises: 1) that grizzlies existed in Labrador, and 2) that the Michelins and other locals didn't know anything about them. The first premise is correct; the second is false. Indeed, as Wright himself conceded, when he'd suggested the possibility to the locals, "they all laughed at that as they were all very familiar with bear tracks."

Wright seemed to ignore every aspect of the eyewitness descriptions that didn't fit his grizzly theory and to focus only on the ones that did. He was, as Sherlock Holmes would say, bending facts to fit theories, rather than theories to fit facts. Still, Professor Wright's idea wasn't all bad: he should get credit for correctly surmising that grizzlies did once roam Labrador, and he was sharpening our own thinking on the matter by his insights. But ultimately the weight of the evidence I think refutes his supposition.

It seemed then, that as Zach and I continued to slowly paddle our way deeper and deeper into the wilderness, we were still no closer to unravelling the mystery.

AGAINST THE CURRENT

So lovely was the loneliness
Of a wild lake, with black rock bound,
And tall pines that tower'd around.
—Edgar Allan Poe, "The Lake," 1827

I STARED OUT FROM MY TENT at the gathering gloom. All around us stood eerie dead trees, which in the darkness felt as if they were silently watching us. Our camping place for the night was far from ideal—the steep banks and alder thickets, combined with muddy shorelines, had limited our options, and we'd had to settle for pitching our tents on a tiny patch of level ground overlooking the water's edge. The river had narrowed considerably, with the opposite bank only a stone's throw away.

Although I'd camped in just about every place imaginable, this hemmed-in little site made me vaguely uneasy. I didn't like the tall, thick bushes immediately beside our tents and how they could conceal anything lurking within them just mere feet from where we slept. To add to our unease, after our fire had burned out, we'd seen across the narrow waterway the eye-shine of some sort of animal watching us. In the darkness it was impossible to guess what it might have been: merely that two glowing eyes had been quietly observing us as we made camp. By the time we'd found a flashlight and aimed it in the direction of the eyes, whatever it was had vanished into the alders.

There'd been plenty of fresh bear and moose tracks along the bank. Normally, fresh bear tracks might put us off sleeping in such a spot, but we'd canoed for hours without coming across anything more promising. Both banks were so steep and thickly overgrown with alders, thorns, and willows that pitching a tent was impossible. We'd landed in a few places, and I'd climbed and clawed my way through the steep embankments to search for anywhere to camp, but without luck. The first place we'd tried revealed nothing but thorn thickets, and the second place had proved no better. With the sun setting, we'd felt grateful enough to find this little patch of sand to spend the night on.

Inside my tent I shivered in my sleeping bag. It promised to be another frosty night. To keep warm, I'd taken to sleeping in my insulated jacket with my hood up, with a sweater on underneath and two layers of pants. My sleeping bag, which had once kept me warm sleeping outdoors even in winter, had lost much of its warmth through frequent use. "I really must," I mumbled while rubbing my arms to keep warm, "invest in a new sleeping bag when this expedition is over."

"What was that?" Zach's voice came through the darkness. He was in his tent next to mine.

"Probably just a bear," I replied.

"Oh okay, I thought you said something."

"Just that I need a new sleeping bag."

"Oh, mine is nice and warm . . . well goodnight," said Zach.

The day had been exhausting; we'd paddled hard against the current all day and had to wade up through several difficult stretches of rapids. At least our exhaustion let us sleep soundly—perhaps a little too soundly. With most of the river's banks dominated by steep slopes filled with thorn thickets, dead trees, and impenetrable alders, this little patch of accessible ground was probably a favourite watering hole for all kinds of animals that climbed down here to drink at the river's edge. Certainly, there were a lot of wildlife tracks around: not only bears and moose but also wolves, beavers, otters, and fishers (a cat-like animal that eats porcupines). I'd set up the trail camera on a big spruce log that had washed ashore and become embedded in the bank. With the camera facing along the river's edge, we felt sure we'd get some interesting recordings overnight.

—

The winding, snaking course of the river demanded every ounce of effort we could muster to overcome its swift current. Meanwhile the ospreys circled overhead as if they were vultures and we were mere walking carrion. If I'd been superstitious, I might have considered it an ill omen how they shrieked and followed us.

As it was, our attention was fixed on battling the river's ever-increasing current. The farther up we ventured, the faster the current became, and the clearer the water. What rendered our task especially difficult was that the alder-infested banks made walking along them while guiding the canoe with rope in the river impossible. Poling, which I'd relied upon on many of my solo journeys, was also impractical given that two people can't stand and pole a fifteen-foot canoe without tipping it, at least not easily; and the banks were impassable thickets, ruling out one of us hiking along the shore while the other poled.

In the bow Zach was paddling like a madman, swinging his paddle with quick, powerful strokes at an almost frantic pace. He'd switched to a bent-shaft paddle, the style favoured by Olympic racers; it features an eight-degree bend at the blade, allowing for increased power and efficiency with each stroke. From the stern with my ultra-light, cherry wood paddle I alternated between forward strokes and jabbing at the bottom whenever it was shallow enough to do so. Every metre of river was a struggle, and if we let up for even a moment we'd lose all momentum and the swirling current would sweep us back downriver.

Fortunately, the river's swift sections sometimes alternated with calmer stretches where we could catch our breath. For food we ate power bars and granola bars. As for water, now that the river had become almost crystal clear, we just filled our bottles directly over the canoe's side. In all my many months of wandering I'd never gotten sick from drinking untreated water in Canada's wilderness. Of course, I made a point of trying not to fill my water bottles downstream of beaver lodges, caribou herds, or other animals.

The calm stretches of river were becoming fewer and fewer. By mid-morning we found ourselves entering a very swift section of narrow, winding river.

"What do you think?" asked Zach from the bow.

I looked at the swirling eddies in the river doubtfully, trying to pick out some path of least resistance. "Well," I said, "I think we might have a chance if we paddle up the left shore."

"Roger that," replied Zach.

We began paddling furiously with short, fast strokes. But it was no use; we were like hamsters on a treadmill, our frantic efforts succeeding only in keeping us at a standstill against the rushing torrent. The river's force soon pushed us sideways into the alder-lined banks. Zach quickly grabbed at the branches, innovating a novel technique on the spot of pulling us upriver branch by branch along the bank. I followed his example, grasping an alder bush to pull on. This unorthodox method worked well enough until we came upon places where the banks had eroded into small bays. Here the alders extended out over the waterline, like mangrove swamps, making it difficult for us to inch by without the current pushing us into the bushes.

Still, we clung and clawed our way forward, battling for every inch. Whenever the current slackened slightly, or the alders receded, we resumed our furious paddling.

Ahead we could hear the roar of bigger rapids. Soon we could see granite boulders looming out of the river like icebergs, with whitewater surging between them.

"We'll have to wade," I said.

"Perfect, my legs could use a stretch," replied Zach.

Along the edge of the river were plenty of rocks and boulders. Taking turns controlling the canoe, we moved elf-like along the rocks, jumping from slippery boulder to slippery boulder. The key, it turned out, was not to lose our footing and smash our heads off the rocks. In places, if the boulders were too far apart, we'd have to cautiously edge into the cold, swirling water, and push the canoe forward that way. We were both wearing hip waders, which allowed us to stay warm and dry, so long as we didn't get knocked off our feet by the rushing current.

To add to our troubles, the wind had been gathering strength, and was now gusting quite strong against us. Zach's broad-brimmed leather hat caught a gust and went flying downriver into rapids, never to be seen again.

"Damn, I loved that hat," he said mournfully.

"You can always get another," I said.

The strong wind gusts, combined with the surging current, slowed our progress down to a crawl. Every inch became a battle to make headway. As we waded into yet another rapid, shuffling our feet along the rocky river bottom while holding onto the canoe for balance, I suddenly plunged into a deep pool. The shock of frigid water surging up to my chest and flooding my waders caused me to exhale. I struggled to find my footing and scamper back onto the safety of a rock. When I managed to climb onto a boulder, I emptied the waders, wrung out my socks, then put them back on. There was no choice but to keep going.

Zach soon joined me in being soaking wet when he slipped and fell off a rock into the river. Fortunately, we had life jackets, and though we were chilled by the icy water, so long as we kept moving we could probably avoid hypothermia.

The river on the other hand wasn't getting any easier. The rapids seemed to be growing steadily larger. Some of the boulders rivalled the size of small cars; we had to climb up and over them while carefully guiding the canoe around. The rapids were occasionally broken by ever-shorter intervals where we could still manage, albeit barely, to paddle hard against the current.

From my seat in the stern, it was sometimes necessary for me to cautiously stand up (technically canoeists aren't supposed to do this), so as to scout out what lay farther upstream and whether to take the left or right bank when confronting another big rapid. Just as I was in the process of doing so, carefully balancing upright in the stern and trying to read the rushing water ahead, a whisky jack swooped out of a dead spruce and flapped mockingly across the water right in front of us. The bird issued a few laughing calls, which felt like it was mocking our predicament and our foolishness in not knowing how to flap our wings and fly.

Neither side of the river looked promising, but we opted for the left shore. We paddled as hard as possible to reach the foot of the rapids, and then, unable to paddle any farther, we climbed onto the rocks. Here there weren't enough boulders to allow us to hop from one to another and stay dry. Instead, the rapids were hemmed in mostly by big alder bushes. This gave the river a claustrophobic feel, with the alders seeming almost as if they were leaning over the water to swallow us up at any moment as we passed below them. We tried to edge into the middle of the river, to get away from the alders, but it proved too deep and drove us back toward the safety of the shore. It seemed we could neither paddle upstream, nor climb along the banks, nor hop along the boulders.

"Looks like our luck has run out," said Zach.

I nodded while studying the river and trying to figure out some way forward. But nothing came to mind. "Well," I said, "I think we're just going to have to get wet."

With one hand on the canoe and the other grasping alder branches, I led the way forward, edging cautiously along.

Scattered along the river bottom, unseen beneath the swirling current, lay rocks and boulders that made tripping easy. The water rose to my knees; a few more steps and it was over my hips, flooding the waders and filling them up. I kept going: there was no other option now. Each step was a struggle against the racing torrent, which threatened to knock us over at any second. The river became deeper still, the frigid water rising to our chests. We tucked as close to the alder bushes as we could; any deeper and we'd be swimming.

Eventually we reached the end of the rapids and had a momentary respite in which to empty our waders and warm ourselves on a rock. But we couldn't rest long; ahead were more rapids, bigger than anything so far. Alongside them towered a huge rock outcrop, looking like some ruined castle tower guarding the river. Zach led the way this time, grabbing the canoe and plunging back down into the frigid river. He powered up the alder-lined bank, grabbing with his right hand at the branches, and with his left dragging the canoe up the rapids. I followed along behind, soaked and chilled to the bone.

Our progress was painfully slow; stumbling forward against the current waist-deep in the water was quickly draining our energy. Still we staggered on for several hundred more metres, until the river curved sharply and a small island broke up the current. Around it were more rapids, but it looked as if we might have a chance to paddle up the right side of them. At any rate, it would give us a much-needed rest from wading and dragging.

We tucked into a little cove amid the alders and climbed soaking wet into the canoe. Then, after taking a moment to catch our breath, we took up our paddles and readied ourselves.

"All right," I said, "let's give it all we've got. If we can make it just beyond these rapids I think things might calm down ahead, at least for a bit."

"Thank the gods," said Zach.

With that, we shoved off from shore and paddled like mad, our frantic strokes driving us through the current. In places where big boulders loomed out of the water, I'd steer us directly in line with them, as they diverted enough water to create a slacker current, allowing us to gain traction. The hard part was when we reached the boulders. We'd have to edge out around them, right into the main force of the rushing waters. Each one of these swift sections was harder than the last, and our arms grew tired from the relentless paddle strokes.

One final stretch of fast-flowing river confronted us before we could reach calmer waters. We were on our knees, paddling with every last ounce of strength at our most furious pace yet. Zach, with the bent-shaft paddle, was practically a human windmill, paddling with tremendous fury. But as he swung his paddle hard for another stroke, it suddenly caught an unseen rock below the waterline. With a crack, the wooden paddle snapped right in two at the bend in the blade.

Zach swore. I reached quickly for our spare paddle, but in the seconds that took, the current overwhelmed us and began spinning the canoe back downriver. Realizing it was hopeless, I steered us into the bank where we could grab onto the alders and regroup.

"Sorry about your paddle," said Zach.

"That's okay. It's not like I had some sort of sentimental attachment to it. I mean, it was only the paddle I took on my four-thousand-kilometre journey alone across Canada's Arctic . . ."

"Oh . . . well, maybe we can glue it back together."

There was no time to think of that, though, and in any case the paddle wasn't to be mended. It had snapped right in two. So Zach took the spare one and we relaunched the canoe. Exhausted and soaking wet, we pushed on and with one last, desperate effort, we at last made it out of the rapids and into calmer water.

The tranquil stretch, it turned out, was only a brief interlude before more rapids roared up ahead. In spite of this our spirits were given a boost by what we could see on the horizon; until now, the thick forests and high banks hemming in the river had concealed anything from view since we'd left the bay. But here there was a break in the treeline, revealing the distant mountains looming over the land.

Maybe it was merely the escape from the claustrophobic feeling of the alders, or perhaps the exhaustion from our hard efforts battling upstream, but to my tired eyes these wild and ancient mountains looked like something out of a fairy tale. Their lower slopes were thickly wooded with spruce and fir while their upper slopes rose to barren, rocky plateaus that stood grey against the blue sky. Scattered across the weathered summits appeared to be immense boulders, which lay haphazardly balanced here and there as if they'd been placed by giants. In reality, melting glaciers ten thousand years ago had likely left them like that. In any case, it was those windswept summits that we were determined to reach.

12

UNKNOWN THINGS

Many a tale the hunters told of their experiences in this silent land . . .
—Edward C. Robinson, *In an Unknown Land*, 1909

"THESE WOODS AND MOUNTAINS are so vast it's easy to see how people might think unknown animals live somewhere out here," remarked Zach in a reflective mood. We were paddling across a comparatively slack section of river, having just passed through more rapids. All around us were dark spruce woods and impenetrable alder thickets.

Zach's observation brought to mind the British explorer Edward C. Robinson's ideas about the Traverspine beast. Robinson, who'd made the earliest record of the mysterious creature back in 1909, had believed it to be some unknown animal species, a possible survivor from the last Ice Age. As Robinson had put it, there was no absolute reason why such beasts should have died out altogether, and if a few should survive, where better than Labrador?

Referred to by scientists as "megafauna," these giant Ice Age mammals are conventionally thought to have gone extinct approximately eleven thousand years ago. But recent paleontology discoveries have revealed that at least one species had in fact endured much longer than that. The last woolly mammoths, it turns out, managed to survive off the coast of Siberia on Wrangel Island until just four thousand years ago—almost seven thousand years later than previously thought. From the perspective of a paleontology timeline, that's about as recent as the blink of an eye.

Among the strange, massive creatures that had once roamed North America were also *Megalonyx*, the giant ground sloth that stood ten feet tall and weighed a ton; a species of moose that had antlers even more gigantic than modern moose; a giant horned muskox (*Bootherium bombifrons*); and even enormous beavers the size of bears (*Castoroides*); not to mention sabre-tooth cats and *Arctodus simus*, the terrifying short-faced bear that stood fourteen feet high on its hind legs. Still, vast as Canada's wilderness is, it seemed unlikely that any of these creatures could have survived into modern times undetected.

The doctors Paddon and Forsyth, both of whom spent many years living in Labrador, had similar thoughts to Robinson about the Traverspine creature. Paddon compared the creature to the yeti, and reasoned that, if the snowy Himalayas might be home to a species of great ape (as he believed), why not Labrador's unexplored mountains? Forsyth also seems to have believed that a two-legged, yeti-like beast stalked Labrador's wilderness.

Although these notions might seem far-fetched today, in the context of the early twentieth century they made considerably more sense. Contrary to what many people might guess, some large mammal species weren't known to science until quite recently. For example, the okapi, a central African forest quadruped that is the closest living relative of the giraffe, had been dismissed as a myth until 1901 when the British explorer Sir Harry Johnston obtained skins and a skull. A similar case is the Komodo dragon, which wasn't recognized by science until 1910. The bonobo or pygmy chimpanzee, which lives in the central African rainforest, was "discovered" only in 1929. Of course, many of these species were known to locals, and had figured more broadly in legends or folklore long before science accepted them as genuine.

So why couldn't the same be true of a Traverspine "gorilla"? The Canadian wilderness, after all, had its own large mammal species that remained unknown to science well into the twentieth century. The Kermode or spirit bear, a rare subspecies of black bear that has white fur and lives in the mist-shrouded rainforests of the Pacific Northwest, stayed hidden from the outside world until 1905. In that year the zoologist William T. Hornaday published his findings documenting what he called the "inland white bear." He gave it the scientific name *Ursus americanus kermodei* after Francis Kermode, a curator at the Provincial Museum of British Columbia who had obtained skins of the bear. Neither Hornaday nor Kermode ever saw a living specimen. Still, after considering all possible explanations for the curious specimens he'd acquired of creamy white fur, teeth, and skulls—and ruling out that they could be from polar bears or albinos, Hornaday wrote, "There is no escape from the conclusion that a hitherto unknown species of white bear, of very small size, inhabits the west-central portion of British Columbia." In other words, an animal that had been dismissed as a legend turned out to be real.

Fascinating as these examples are, Zach and I were nevertheless in general agreement that, when put down on paper and analyzed objectively, it was virtually impossible to think that a large animal species could have survived in Canada undetected into the modern era. The harsh conditions across the northern wilderness meant much lower levels of biodiversity than in tropical rainforests, where in modern times most new mammal discoveries have taken place. More importantly, although a few individuals could undoubtedly avoid detection in the millions of square miles of Canada's wilderness, for an entire species to survive there'd have to be at least a breeding-sized population. At minimum, that would mean nearly a hundred individuals to reproduce successfully and sustain the species. Given the centuries of fur trapping, hunting, and exploration undertaken in Canada's remote hinterlands, it's hard to believe that's possible. Ultimately, as far as the Traverspine mystery was concerned, it seemed to us that an explanation based on some existing creature in the animal kingdom, like a mangy polar bear or rare barren-land grizzly, was far more plausible.

Then again, in 1992 the scientific world was astonished by the discovery of a new animal species in the inaccessible highlands of northern Vietnam. On an expedition there, a team of scientists found the remains of a mysterious antelope-like goat creature, which subsequent analysis confirmed to be an unknown bovid species. The scientists returned to the highlands to search for further evidence of the creature. But it wasn't until 1999 that a motion-activated trail camera managed to capture an image of a live one. The new species was named saola, meaning "spindle-horned," a reference to the animal's exceptionally long horns.

Sightings of this elusive animal remain extremely infrequent, and not until 2010 did someone succeed for the first time in tracking one down in person in the wild and documenting it. They remain one of the world's rarest and least known creatures.

So perhaps anything is possible. Indeed, in 2003 a team of scientists on the wild slopes of volcanic mountains in Tanzania in East Africa made another shocking discovery. The scientists had scaled the mountains to investigate reports of a strange primate known as the "kipunji." They assumed, quite naturally, that it would turn out to be entirely fictional—a mere local legend of a mythical beast. Then, in forests some six thousand feet above sea level, one of the members spotted a ghost-like monkey perched in a tree high above; it stood about three feet tall and had silverish-brown fur, a dark face, and a prominent tuft of hair at the top of its head. Incredibly, it was a kipunji—the myth, it turned out, was no myth. The new species, formally classified for the first time in 2005, was given the scientific name *Rungwecebus kipunji*. These mysterious monkeys were a completely new genus, conclusively disproving the notion that, in the twenty-first century, no animals could possibly remain unknown to science. Nor was this the only new primate to come to light in recent years. In 2007 another astonishing discovery made headlines when scientists found a new monkey species deep in the mists of the Congo rainforest, which was named the lesula.

It's not only in Africa or Asia that unknown animals have recently come to light. For the first time in decades, in 2013 a new species of carnivorous mammal was discovered in the Western Hemisphere. High in the cloud forests of the Andes Mountains in South America, a previously unknown species of tree-dwelling carnivore was found. The new species was christened the olinguito, which have long furry tails and are distantly related to raccoons. They're nocturnal creatures, living only in mist-shrouded trees in remote mountains, which helps explain what kept them hidden for so long. Quite a few other mammal species have also been discovered in the twenty-first century by scientists, ranging from several new lemur species in Madagascar to tree-dwelling giant rats in the South Pacific, to a new monkey species deep in the Amazon jungle. Simply put, even today our world remains a much more mysterious place than most of us realize, with plenty of space for unknown things to stay hidden.

Labrador, too, is incomparably wilder and less populated than any of these places. Indeed, Tanzania, where the kipunji was discovered, has a population density of sixty-seven people per square kilometre; Labrador in contrast is a mere 0.092. In other words, Tanzania has more than 728 times as many people per square kilometre than Labrador, and yet still has space for animal species to remain hidden. That there are other unknown species as yet undiscovered lurking in the world's remotest wilderness areas is a given—just how many no one knows. Some scientists think the true number of unknown mammals (let alone reptiles, insects, fish, and so forth) may run into the hundreds.

I drew a stroke of my wooden paddle through the water. We were in a big bend of the river, where the current had mellowed enough for us to paddle. A few ducks, mostly mergansers and pintails, swam across the water up ahead. I scanned the dark woods on either bank, wondering what unguessed mysteries these ancient forests might hold.

"From my living room it seems impossible, but actually being here, surrounded on all sides by dense forests, hell, there could be a sasquatch for all I know," said Zach.

"I once tried to calculate how many square kilometres of wilderness Canada has," I said. "It's something like five or six million."

"That's a hell of a lot," replied Zach.

I nodded. I'd heard stories firsthand from Indigenous hunters familiar with the vast subarctic swamps covering millions of hectares around James Bay who'd come across strange tracks in the soft moss. The tracks, they said, were large and half-human looking. One of the hunters, who I came to know better, described a sighting he'd once had on the outskirts of town of a large, hairy type of creature that appeared to walk on only two legs in thick brush. I'd always taken such accounts with a grain of salt, but I didn't for a moment doubt that those who told me these stories genuinely believed them.

"The stat that always gets me," I said, "is that Canada has so many lakes that even today no geographer knows just how many there are. Around three million is the best guess anyone's come up with."

"Not to mention all the unexplored mountain caves," added Zach. "There must be thousands."

On the other hand, the local trappers around Traverspine seemed to have had something quite different in mind with regard to the creatures that had terrified them into sleeping with doors barred and upstairs with axes and guns. They were convinced it was something supernatural—the devil or "one of his agents" in Merrick's words.

13

THE LAND OF SHADOWS

It is absolutely necessary, for the peace and safety of mankind, that some of earth's dark, dead corners and unplumbed depths be left alone.
—H.P. Lovecraft, *At the Mountains of Madness*, 1936

AFTER NAVIGATING UP another long stretch of rocky rapids that lasted nearly a kilometre, which left us soaked and chilled to the bone, we resolved at last to give up any attempt to push on farther by canoe. The river was becoming too wild and swift for upstream travel to be practical. My left wader had sprung numerous leaks and ripped quite badly, and even the waterproof neoprene I wore underneath had apparently punctured, rendering my waders heavy and weighed down with water every step I took. Zach was in a similarly drenched and chilled condition. With darkness coming on we decided to make camp, but the thick, impenetrable woods on either bank made doing so difficult.

In the middle of the river, which was churned up by rapids, lay a small island. The island was a wild tangle of dead trees, blown over and criss-crossed every which way by fierce windstorms. To add to the island's frightful appearance, it seemed as if during the spring floods large amounts of drifting spruce trees and other logs had smashed into it and were now heaped up across it. Besides all this deadfall, nearly every inch of the island appeared covered in dense thorns or alder thickets. It was, in short, just about the most unpromising-looking campsite I'd ever seen. But we were sufficiently desperate that the island seemed enticing enough to tired eyes and wearied limbs.

To reach the island's shore we paddled against the swift current to the middle of the river, then landed on a steep, uninviting bank. It took some effort to balance and climb out, then claw our way over deadfall, alders, and thorns onto solid ground. If the island had looked uninviting from the water, it seemed even more so now that we were standing on it. Thorns tore at us from every direction, and we couldn't find a single spot of level ground anywhere big enough to put a tent on. Fallen spruce trees, hollows, depressions, and small hummocks riddled the island. The only positive was the abundant raspberries and red currants, which we happily devoured.

"Well," I said, "I don't think we can camp here."

"No," agreed Zach.

"On the other hand, we probably won't find anything better if we push on."

"Probably not," agreed Zach.

It was a conundrum. I wandered over to the edge of the island, climbing over some deadfall to get a better view of the river's opposite shore. As far as camping places went, there didn't appear to be anything over there either, as high, steep banks a hundred feet or more towered above the water.

But there was a smaller stream draining down into the river. We'd earlier noticed this stream on our topographic maps; our plan had been to follow it, if possible, to the foot of the mountains, which were still some five or six kilometres away. The sight of the dark waters of a wild stream swirling down from forested mountains had always exercised an almost hypnotic allure on me. So I figured we might as well leave the island and try cutting across in the canoe to the stream—where we might have more luck finding a spot to bed down for the night. Zach agreed.

We returned through the thorns and alders to the canoe and paddled wearily across the river to where the stream, roaring over boulders and rocks, tumbled into the main river. Not far up from its outlet a big spruce had toppled across its width, blocking our view of what lay beyond. But from what we could see it looked like the stream was enclosed by high, thickly wooded banks. Near its mouth, where we hovered in the current in the canoe, the hills were even higher and steeper, rising almost vertically above the river.

Once we'd landed on the bank our camping prospects seemed even worse than what they'd been on the island, given that the high, wooded hills ran nearly straight down to the river. With our options limited and the sun going down, I decided to climb a nearby hill as quickly as I could to scout things out while Zach stayed behind with the canoe.

In all my adventures I don't think I'd ever encountered such difficult terrain before; along with alder thickets and thorns, barriers of deadfall were everywhere, with sharp, protruding branches that were easy to catch on. The ground was soft and covered in thick sphagnum moss, which I sank into with every step, making it difficult to gain traction; it was like trying to run with giant wet sponges strapped to my feet. Still, I clawed and climbed my way over the deadfall, weaving up and over the logs, grabbing onto twisted spruces and firs to pull myself up, step by step, to the summit.

When I finally reached the crest of the hill my hopes were dashed: instead of the level ground I'd been counting on, the summit was the same wildly uneven terrain, cratered with moss and lichen-filled depressions, with deadfall and trees everywhere. Pitching a tent here would be out of the question. I tried to poke through the branches to gain a view of the river far below. I couldn't see Zach or the canoe, concealed as they were by thickets. But the blur of whitewater roaring in the river below, as well as the tangled island, I could make out plainly. Everywhere I looked there was nothing but thick, dark woods and steep hills.

Having failed to find anything promising on top, I decided to take a different route back. I cut down the eastern side of the hill to see if I might meet with more luck there. This led me in the direction of the snaking course of the tributary stream. When I reached the bottom, there were only alder thickets and more deadfall. In desperation I pushed on, jumping over fallen logs and weaving through dead spruces until at last I came to an area that was slightly less dense. The ground here was as uneven as elsewhere, and covered in fallen logs and balsam fir saplings. But it was marginally less thick than anywhere else we'd seen so far, and with no better options, this place would have to do. I hurried back to Zach at a jogging pace, pushing through bushes and jumping over logs, until, half exhausted, I stumbled out of the thicket and found him on the river's edge.

"Find anything?" he asked.

"Well . . . it definitely won't be our best campsite ever. But I think we can make it work if we do a bit of structural engineering."

"Engineering?"

"There's some dead trees we're going to have to chop down or knock over to clear enough space to put up our tents."

"Right," said Zach.

The thicket I'd crossed to get back to the river was too dense to try to portage all our gear through, so instead we plunged back into the water and together waded and hauled the canoe up the stream. The cold, swirling water rose almost to our hips, but we struggled up the side and then wove around the big fallen spruce tree, before cutting back across to the bank, trying our best not to lose our balance in the swollen rapids.

It took our combined efforts to heave and haul our gear up out of the stream and through barricades of fallen trees into the woods. Just as I was hauling my heavy backpack up, I took another step and suddenly fell right through some tangled roots and dead branches to a hollow below.

"Are you all right?" asked Zach, looking down from above.

"Yeah. My body broke the fall," I said. I was a little bruised, but otherwise unhurt. The deadfall and tangled branches, heaped and tumbled every which way, had concealed a natural opening where the water in the stream had carved away and undercut the banks, making an ideal booby trap. I climbed out and onto more solid ground.

We pushed inland a short distance, where I pointed out to Zach the none-too-promising spot I'd seen earlier. It was little more than a thicket of dead spruces, with sharp branches sticking out every which way on which it would be easy to poke one's eye out. The ground was uneven and sloped up away from the stream, with lots of shrubs and thorny raspberry bushes. The closest thing to level ground, which covered no more than three feet, was wet and muddy.

"Okay." Zach nodded. "I think I can see how this would work."

"That's the spirit."

After hauling our canoe up the steep bank and through the thicket, we set about clearing a small space for our tents. First we knocked over some dead trees by pushing on them; then we chopped down a few others with the hatchet. Zach hauled a number of logs out of the way, while I uprooted as many thorn bushes as possible along the ground. That done, we selected our tent sites. Zach opted for the more sloped ground a little farther inland, while I settled for the muddier but more level patch. To deal with the mud, I laid down some balsam fir boughs. The thick moss and fallen debris made staking down tents a bit difficult, since the pegs didn't find much to dig into, so instead we relied on guy lines lashed to dead spruces to keep them up. We were both slightly apprehensive that any number of the dead spruces, with their sharp branches, might blow down in the night and impale or crush us.

But as with everything, there's always an upside, and the upside of this place was that we had no trouble finding ample firewood. When we'd taken care of our tents and laid out our sleeping bags, we made a nice warming fire in a little depression nearby, and hung up our soaked clothing in the dead spruce branches to dry. Zach meanwhile decided to try his luck with fishing.

While Zach disappeared off through the thicket in the direction of the water, I pulled out my topographic maps and sat examining them on a spruce log near the fire. The stream we'd camped beside seemed to originate from a lake high in the mountains. Judging from what I could make out on the map, it looked like vast swamps and muskegs along with more thickly wooded hills separated us from the start of mountains. The stream, with its windy course and many bends, probably wasn't worth trying to follow too closely, especially since alongside its bank were sure to be dense thickets. But we could use it as a point of reference as we scaled the hills and cut across the swamps, making our way on foot to the mountains. It might help keep us from getting lost in these trackless and lonely forests. Once we reached the mountains, we'd climb the highest peak we could and search for any caves. If a Traverspine gorilla really did exist, I figured a mountain cave is where it'd be found.

Just then I thought I heard something over my shoulder. I cast a sudden glance at the spruces and bushes around me. The dead trees, with their twisted branches, looked rather eerie, almost like frowning figures reaching out to grab me when my back was turned. I sat listening for a few moments, but the stream's rushing waters made it difficult to distinguish any other sounds, or to tell if anything had moved near the camp. The thickness of the black spruces and fallen trees that lay toppled everywhere created a suffocating atmosphere, especially since it made it easy for anything or anyone to creep up on us undetected. I broke some branches off the spruce log I was sitting on and tossed them into the fire, kindling a bigger blaze.

Then I went and strapped the trail camera onto a big fir at the edge of the little clearing we'd made, facing it out from camp toward the deep woods. This sure felt like a spot where some animal would try to creep noiselessly up on our tents in the darkness.

To make it on foot to the mountains we'd have to leave behind everything non-essential, including the canoe, paddles, watertight barrel, and extra food. On an overland trek, especially through dense bush, we'd be able to take only the bare necessities: our tents, backpacks, survival gear, as well as food rations for several days. The trail camera, which was a bit heavy, would have to stay behind. But we could leave it turned on and lashed to the tree the entire time we were away. Quite likely something might come along while we were gone, rip open our barrel, and devour the rest of our food rations.

Returning to the fire, I was beginning to wonder what had happened to Zach. He'd been gone for quite a while, and I was starting to get an uneasy feeling. Accustomed as I was to mostly solo journeys, I wasn't entirely used to having to deal with the anxiety of worrying about a companion in the wilderness. In my mind I pictured Zach fishing along the slippery rocks of the river, and slipping and smashing his head off one, leaving him face-down in the current. Or, with his back turned while reeling in a trout, a bear sneaking up on him from behind. Our sole can of bear spray was still resting in the canoe; neither of us actually bothered to carry it, preoccupied as we usually were with just figuring out a path through the rough terrain. "Well," I thought to myself, "I'm sure he's fine. He does beat people up for money, after all."

At that moment the alder bushes began to sway and shake immediately in front of me. Something was moving through them. I sprang to my feet—only to see Zach emerge out of the thicket.

"I was just beginning to wonder what happened to you," I said, poking casually at the fire with a stick.

"Sorry, I ended up hiking down to the main river to try my luck there."

"Did you catch anything?"

"Nothing," replied Zach. "I saw plenty of brook trout, about six or seven inches long, which followed my lures, but they wouldn't bite. If I had more time I likely could have caught one, but with it getting dark I figured I'd best head back."

"That was probably wise."

"To tell you the truth, I had kind of an uneasy feeling," Zach continued, taking a seat by the fire and warming his hands. "It occurred to me that with the noise of the water I wouldn't be able to hear anything stalking me through the woods, and with the bush so thick I certainly wouldn't see it. It'd be easy to wander too close to the forest edge and just get grabbed and hauled into it while your back is turned."

I nodded. "Very easy."

Without the benefit of fresh trout, we made do with our freeze-dried meals, boiling water over the fire and cooking two of them. By the time they were ready, the sun had sunk below the horizon, leaving the woods dark and gloomy. We sat by the flickering firelight eating and warming ourselves.

In the darkness the woods felt even more unnerving, with the shadows cast by the firelight making the dead spruces seem as if they were leaning in toward us. Our wet clothing hanging in the branches looked in the gloom like monstrous forms had encircled us.

"Do you know what a windigo is?" I asked, crouching near the blaze.

Zach looked up at me. "A shapeshifter who eats people? And I think eating people can also turn you into one?"

"Sort of," I said. "According to Algonquian legend, it's a demon or evil spirit that lurked in deep, dark northern forests, preying upon people who foolishly ventured there and eating them. Some legends say it was a kind of giant, hideous, vaguely human monster, others that it possessed people and turned them into cannibals."

"Well, that's a nice thought to fall asleep with," said Zach.

The fire burned low. With our flashlights we picked our way over the fallen spruces to our tents. Zach picked up the broken paddle, which was sharp and jagged where it had snapped, and took it into his tent with him. All things considered, sleeping with a wooden stake seemed like a prudent idea. Inside my tent I crawled into my sleeping bag, shivering in the cold, then switched off my flashlight. The clouded sky concealed the half moon, leaving us in total darkness.

14

HORROR IN THE WOODS

The wind through the trees is the windigo, the sigh of restless souls.
—Richard Morenus, *Crazy-White-Man*
(Sha-ga-na-she Wa-du-kee), 1952

L YING IN MY TENT in the pitch dark, my mind drifted to still darker places. I thought of some of the things I'd read about windigos. Northern Indigenous oral histories as well as the diaries and letters of fur traders are replete with references to this mysterious monster. No two descriptions agree exactly on the nature of the windigo, and even the word itself has been spelled dozens of different ways. Most historical accounts describe it as an "evil spirit" that could possess human beings, but some say that it could also take a physical form of its own.

Based on reports given by Atikamekw elders in northern Quebec in the 1920s, the anthropologist Richard Preston provided one of the most detailed descriptions:

The Witiko ... are solitary, aggressive cannibals, naked but impervious to cold, with black skin covered by resin-glued sand. They have no lips, large crooked teeth, hissing breath, and big bloodshot eyes, something like owls' eyes. Their feet are more than two feet long, with long, pointed heels, and have only one big toe: "This is the way his tracks appear on sand and snow." Fingers and fingernails are "like the claws of the great mountain bears." The voice is strident, reverberating, and drawn-out into howls, and his "food was rotten wood, swamp moss, mushrooms, corpses, and human flesh." Witiko has extraordinary strength and is invulnerable. He is a nocturnal hunter of men; when he is close, his heart beats twice as quickly with joy, sounding like the drumming of a grouse. They can fly and swim under water . . .

I thought it somewhat strange that none of the chroniclers who'd reported on Traverspine had suggested the possibility that the creature might have been a windigo. There were, after all, some notable parallels. Besides the general similarities of it being a large, frightening, inhuman thing that appeared out of dark woods, there were more specific resemblances. Professor Wright had said that the Traverspine creatures had torn up rotten logs looking for food, something native elders reported windigos did. There was also the apparent targeting of children, the strange tracks, and the whispering noise that Robinson had noted the beast made, which is not unlike traditional descriptions of the windigo's eerie, hissing call.

Some authorities on the windigo, such as Samuel Makidemewabe, a Cree elder from northern Manitoba, believed that originally all windigos were once human, but that after they tasted human flesh they gradually lost their humanity, eventually degenerating into hideous, subhuman creatures. However, the Omushkego elder Louis Bird held that some windigos may never have been human. Bird explained it this way in his oral history of the Omushkego:

> Wihtigo. It was something that happened among humans. It means an other-than-human was created from an ordinary human—and sometimes maybe not. There is a question there. There were many kinds. There is a wihtigo that was created by starvation—humans starved, went crazy, and ate human flesh . . . Other wihtigos are not understood—it is not known where they came from.

This ambiguity reflects the terror and mystery of the windigo, a creature that was so disturbing and horrifying it was often considered unwise to even speak of it. The explorer David Thompson, regarded as one of the greatest mapmakers who ever lived, believed that windigos were an "evil spirit." Thompson claimed to have personally witnessed at least two incidents of windigo possession, both of which resulted in executing the person in question for fear they'd turn into a cannibal if not stopped. The fur trader George Nelson also witnessed what he believed were cases of windigo possession. Nelson described it as "a sort of mania, or fever, a distemper of the brain." In his diary, he noted that the victim's eyes were "wild and uncommonly clear—they seem as if they glistened." Another fur trader, Charles McKenzie, in 1837 bore witness to a mass panic sparked by the supposed appearance of a windigo in what is now northwestern Ontario. Over a hundred Ojibwa fled in terror to McKenzie's trading post on Lac Seul for protection. Armed guards were posted in the woods for over a week, and a medicine man engaged in con-juring to ward off the evil creature. McKenzie reported that the Ojibwa who'd seen the creature described it as covered in hair and, curiously, as leaving huge footprints that lacked heels.

Whatever had happened at McKenzie's post sounded like it had certain similarities to what transpired at Traverspine. Just like at McKenzie's post, at Traverspine the whole com-munity and the nearby lumber camp at Mud Lake had turned out with guns to patrol the woods and hunt whatever had made the strange tracks. Modern skeptics might perhaps won-der if mass hysteria had caused these cases, similar to what happened at Salem with its infamous witch trials. It seems that these small, isolated communities, deeply religious and under stress from circumstances imposed by harsh environ-ments, were prone to wild rumours that triggered outbreaks of collective fear. In another case from Labrador in the early 1900s, a family were reportedly "scared stiff" and fled in ter-ror from an isolated valley where they lived because a wind-igo had supposedly appeared in the area. The anthropologist Richard Preston, who in the 1970s did fieldwork among Cree communities in the subarctic forests of neighbouring north-ern Quebec, noted in his research that "actual Witiko scares are a part of the experience of many Northern Algonkians of middle age or older. These are often related to the mystery and great concern over lost persons or may be a more complicated matter of group terror."

This fear was shared by the French Canadian voyageurs who were tasked with paddling the lonely rivers of the Canadian back-woods transporting furs. The voyageurs dreaded encountering the windigo on a portage or camping place, or anywhere else they might be ambushed. It was said by the early fur trade historian George Bryce that:

> No crew would push on after the sun was set, lest they should see this apparition. Some said he was a spirit condemned to wander to and fro on the earth on account of crimes committed, others believed the Wendigo was a desperate outcast, who had tasted human flesh, and prowled about at night, seeking in the camping-places of traders a victim. Tales were told of unlucky trappers who had disappeared in the woods and had never been heard of again.

A glimpse into what these spine-tingling encounters with a windigo might have been like was offered by the explorer Henry Youle Hind, a nineteenth-century geologist and professor at the University of Toronto. In the 1850s Hind ventured deep into the Labrador wilderness. Hind's guides told him that the windigo was a giant monster that stalked the subarctic forests:

> The Indian sat looking at the fire for many minutes. I did not want to interrupt his thoughts.... At length he spoke, looking at the body, and pointing to it, saying, "He said last winter that some one would die before the year was out."
>
> I knew well enough that it was one of their superstitions that had troubled him... So I said to him, "Did he see anything?"
>
> "He came across tracks."
>
> "Tracks?"
>
> "A Windigo," said the Indian.

"Have you ever seen one?" I asked him.

"I have seen tracks."

"Where?"

"On the St. Marguerite, the Mingan, the Manitou, the Oa-na-ma-ne. My cousin saw tracks on the Manitou last winter, and he said to me and many of us, 'Something will happen.'"

"What were the tracks like?" I said to him.

"Windigoes," he replied.

"Well, but how big were they?"

He looked at me and said nothing, nor would he speak on the subject again.

"These Montagnais think," continued Pierre [one of Hind's guides], "that the Windigoes are giant cannibals, twenty and thirty feet high. They think that they live on human flesh, and that many Indians who have gone hunting, and have never afterwards been heard of, have been devoured by Windigoes."

It was darkly fascinating to consider that even the Montagnais thought there was something sinister lurking in the vast sub-arctic wilds of Labrador.

Certain aspects of Professor Hind's account, written in the late 1850s, about a half century before what happened at Traverspine, also seem to mirror it. In particular there is the emphasis placed on the finding of mysterious tracks. Unfortunately, Hind's guides didn't provide more detail of what the windigo tracks were supposed to look like—almost as if they were afraid to speak too much about it. Other fur trade sources and Indigenous elders state that windigo tracks were large, about a foot long, tapering to a point on either end. The tracks at

Traverspine were similarly described as being large, but with the added detail that they included a cloven hoof—something more often associated with the Judeo-Christian tradition of demons or the Devil than the Algonquian windigo.

In 1949 the Cree teacher Edward Ahenakew transcribed a discussion he'd had with the elder Weipust, who was born sometime in the mid-1800s. "There is no doubt," Weipust told him, "that Wetikoos existed in the old days"—specifically, said Weipust, in the most northern parts of the subarctic, like Labrador, where conditions were harsh and hunting often unsuccessful, and when a lone family might occasionally suffer famine. As Weipust explained, a hunter in this situation starts to find that:

> his luck leaves him, everything goes wrong, he can kill nothing, maybe the animals migrate to some other region. He goes out to hunt every day, trying to feed his starving family and himself. Their plight becomes desperate . . . a person will do almost anything to secure food. As days of fasting go by; hope dies and despair takes its place. A time comes when one of the party begins to look longingly though slyly at another. The person is being sorely tempted to kill, so as to eat. It becomes an obsession . . . At last—chance offering, it happens. The person kills and soon he (or she) is eating. He has passed from being a human being to beastliness. The rest of the family realize that they have a Wetikoo to cope with. All that they have heard about such monsters comes into their minds. A great dread overwhelms them, the marrow inside the bones seems to melt and they have no power to

move or fight. While they might have met ordinary dangers bravely, they were as frightened children in the presence of a powerful inhuman monster. They give in and very soon share the fate of the first victim.

Weipust also said that a person could become a windigo through being cursed by an "evil spirit" that might appear in a dream. Ahenakew, who recorded Weipust's story, mentioned in his notes that he "accepted his words as of great value . . . To continue it is said that once a person has tasted human flesh he loses all human instincts, and he turns into a fierce carnivorous beast yearning to prey on his kind. He is gifted with super-natural powers."

A few incidents similar to those described by Weipust are attested in the historical record as having actually occurred in Labrador. The surveyor Albert Peter Low, a hard-headed geologist with little patience for ghost stories, nevertheless did note in his report on Labrador hearing about a tragic case involving three families whose members had perished from starvation—a case that seemed to have eventually led to cannibalism. Dr. Paddon, without mentioning the windigo by name, also noted in his memoir a strange ghost story he'd heard that seems to have all the hallmarks of a windigo:

Two men, father and son, who have never had any troubles elsewhere, found an iron pot, old and abandoned but still quite serviceable, at a very old Indian camping place, which they adopted and took . . . They used the pot to cook a meal and lay down to rest. The younger man felt as if someone was trying to stifle him, and the elder man too was conscious of a sinister presence … Anyhow, they got out, but later on they tried again with the same results, and a barely used tilt [a small cabin] has been abandoned and even part of the hunting ground, and no one will use it or camp near it.

Later, they heard the story of that pot from some Indians. Many years earlier, a party of hungry Indians was struggling towards North West River trading post. A married woman gave out and was left in camp with one or more children. As soon as possible, the husband came back with food and found his squaw alone, insane and with abundant evidence of cannibalism. In terror he shot her, and the remains were buried nearby. The Indians would never use the pot which had been used in this ghastly tragedy, but the trappers had ignorantly taken and used it.

Although Paddon doesn't seem to have known about windigos, the story he recorded seems to fit with traditional beliefs about them. From the point of view of a believer, it would seem that the "evil spirit" had waited until the old woman was alone and vulnerable, before possessing her and turning her into a cannibal. After she'd been killed, the windigo spirit somehow remained attached or associated with the iron cooking pot she had apparently used to cook the children in.

It's easy to think that rare cases of cannibalism might have happened in a place like Labrador, given how difficult conditions could be, especially in the depths of the long, dark winter. But an actual thirty-foot monster with glowing red eyes seemed harder to believe in. At least, I didn't particularly wish to believe in it while lying in the dark in my sleeping bag, surrounded on all sides by thick woods. Could the fear and stress of starvation, or the isolation of the northern solitudes, have caused people to hallucinate a windigo? Or maybe the belief in a supernatural monster was merely the human mind's attempt to come to terms with the darkest horrors perpetrated by humans themselves?

It seems an interesting coincidence that virtually every northern forest–based culture had some version of a cannibalistic being that lived in deep, dark woods. The Germanic peoples had their legends of witch-eating cannibals; Eastern Europeans had Baba Yaga; in the Carpathian Mountains tales were told of vampires; Scandinavian folklore held that the north woods were home to hideous flesh-eating trolls. Maybe the Traverspine beast had been a kind of local Labradorian variant? A sort of cultural metaphor meant to warn people of the dangers of straying too far off the beaten path? Or maybe it was the very forest itself—the shadowy, mystical-seeming landscape with its ancient evergreen trees, verdant moss, hanging lichens, and rainy atmosphere—that made people prone to imagining things? Certainly, I found it easy to do so whenever I looked at the deep, dark, silent woods all around.

In any case, in spite of some similarities, it didn't seem as if the Traverspine beast or beasts fit with a windigo. None of the witnesses or chroniclers had compared it to such, and at least a few of them, living as they did in Labrador, must have been familiar with windigo legends. They'd instead interpreted it as belonging to different category of being: either an unknown animal species (Forsyth, Paddon, Grenfell), a survivor from the last Ice Age (Robinson), a barren-land grizzly (Wright), or the devil or a demon (Merrick). That last interpretation, the devil or a demon, was what the local settlers had apparently believed.

I rolled over and pulled the sleeping bag tighter around me.

15

CROSSING THE DIVIDE

The woods are lovely, dark and deep.
—Robert Frost, "Stopping by Woods on a Snowy Evening," 1923

T HE UNCERTAINTIES OF the night dissipated in the clear light of morning. The day had dawned warm and sunny. Zach and I crawled out of our tents to find our camp, insofar as we could tell, undisturbed. The sunny skies raised our spirits, and gave us confidence that we could navigate through the thick woods to the foot of the mountains.

For breakfast we ate granola bars and drank green tea from our thermoses. Our gear we sorted through, leaving aside any items we could do without. These we stashed in the barrel, taking enough food out of it to last us three days or so. The canoe we tied securely to a big spruce. This may have been a bit paranoid on our part, but neither of us wanted to take even the slightest chance that a windstorm or landslide or some other unforeseen event might knock it into the rapids and then have the river sweep it away, stranding us here. Stranger things had happened in Labrador, after all. The trail camera we left pointed at the food barrel in the centre of the clearing we'd made.

With that, we set off. We began by climbing uphill, picking our way over deadfall and weaving around sharp snapped-off spruce branches. The woods were so thick it was impossible to see more than a few feet in any direction. Within sixty seconds of leaving our camp, it seemed as if it had vanished into the forest, so completely did the dense woods hide any trace of it. The warm weather meanwhile had conjured up, as if by black magic, legions of blackflies and mosquitoes, which attacked our necks and faces. Given the thick terrain and complete absence of anything resembling a path, it was impossible to swat the bugs away, as our hands were needed just to wrestle branches out of the way as we hiked.

Things had been challenging enough the day before when I'd ascended a hill to look for a place to camp. But now, with our heavy packs weighing us down, weaving through the thickets was utterly exhausting. Every few steps our packs would snag on a fallen spruce as we attempted to duck under it, or else a clawing branch would catch one of the straps. Despite the fact that we were headed uphill, with each step our boots sank into the thick green moss that smothered every inch of ground.

By the time we reached the crest of the hill, we were panting and sweating heavily, the sweat mixed with blood from blackfly and mosquito bites. I'd donned a mesh bug net before leaving camp that afforded me some slight protection, though it made seeing more difficult, and inevitably some blackflies found a way through. Zach meanwhile suffered terribly, as he was without any net. Nor had we bothered to pack any bug spray, given that it was September and normally cold enough that mosquitoes and blackflies weren't an issue.

"This warm weather is brutal—I'd take the cold any day," said Zach, wiping his brow and swatting blackflies as he leaned against a twisted spruce.

"At least we don't have to worry about hypothermia," I said, slouching exhausted against a fir.

From the crest of the hill we could see the tortuous course of the stream, winding its lonely way through thickets of dead spruces, and hemmed in on all sides by steep, forested hills. Looming abruptly in the distance were the mountains. In a straight line they were about three and a half kilometres away. But to walk in a straight line here was impossible; the thickets, deadfall, and swamps would necessitate frequent detours, and in the end, we'd be lucky if we kept the total distance down to five or six kilometres. We set as our objective a tall, craggy, barren peak. Immediately to the northeast of it there was a cleft in the mountains, where, we guessed, the stream must run down. If we could make it there, with any luck it might allow us to gain a foothold and avoid the steep cliffs on the mountain face.

"What do you think?" I asked Zach.

"It sure looks like a place where some kind of wood ape might live," he replied, only half jokingly.

We pushed on from the hill, since resting only allowed the blackflies to attack us more freely. Climbing down the hill wasn't much easier than climbing up; thorn thickets clawed at us, while we had to put our feet down with care, as the spongy moss might gave way, and twisting an ankle was all too easy. By the time we reached the bottom, the mountains were completely hidden from view, and if not for the sun, we wouldn't have known which way to head. A wilderness of deadfall confronted us in all directions.

Getting lost would be easy if we relied on a compass or a GPS. A compass would be useless given the thickets, and trying to stare at a tiny GPS screen would have meant tripping over all the fallen trees and roots. Instead we set our course by the sun, heading southwest. The sun, I think, is the easiest and most reliable means of navigating when in dense brush. It was almost the fall equinox, which fortunately happens to be one of only two days a year when the sun truly rises exactly due east (the other is the spring equinox). The rest of the year it rises various degrees off from east, depending on the date and the latitude. In northern Canada, if you're close to the winter solstice, the sun rises close to southeast, and at the summer solstice, close to northeast. The rest of the year it's moving between these positions; how much depends on latitude. But regardless of the time of the year, if you're north of the Tropic of Cancer (and everywhere in Canada is), at solar noon the sun will always be exactly due south. Keeping this in mind, a person can more or less orient themselves as they hike by the position of the sun relative to themselves and the time of the day. Therefore, as long as you're mindful of the sun's position throughout the day, you shouldn't lose your way.

My pants tore on several dead spruce branches as I wove between them, but, so Zach informed me, ripped pants were the fashion nowadays anyway. We kept at it, hacking, clawing, weaving, and trekking onward, all the while swarmed by blackflies and mosquitoes. Our faces were soon scratched by the spruce branches, which kept smacking us in the face as we passed them by. Our shins, too, took a beating on all the fallen spruce trees we were constantly bumping into, hidden as they were by thickets of raspberry thorns. On the plus side, we were able to snack frequently on all the raspberries, bunchberries, and lingonberries we were encountering.

"It seems to be getting thicker," said Zach, pushing a branch aside.

"I think we're coming up to a little stream, judging by the alders," I replied. Alders flourish wherever there's water, so it seemed some kind of stream was likely to be nearby.

"Good, I could use a refill on my water bottle."

The bushes grew steadily thicker, and we were soon practically crawling over alders and through them. The foliage had become so dense that even though Zach and I were only a few feet apart, in places we could barely see each other. I took another blind step, only to find there wasn't any ground beneath my feet, causing me to plunge forward into a hidden hollow.

"Are you all right?" said Zach, coming up from behind.

"Yeah . . . I think I found the stream."

The alders, it turned out, were growing right across the stream, smothering every inch of it. They had concealed where in the spring the high water must have eroded the banks enough to create the depression I'd stumbled into. But the stream was now little more than a tiny, suffocated trickle, too shallow to fill a bottle in. I'd fallen straight into it, but fortunately the alders had mostly broken my fall, and I was unhurt. Picking myself back up, I tunnelled through the jungle of alders, ducking under their interlocked branches until I came out into more dead spruces on the other side. A few moments later Zach emerged from the thicket and we resumed our trek.

As morning passed into afternoon, we seemed to be getting no closer to the mountains; it felt as if we were merely wandering aimlessly in the thickets. It made us appreciate the troubles that J.M. Scott, the earlier explorer, had faced when he'd tried to reach the mountains on foot. He'd given up after three days of hopeless wandering. Our clothing was becoming ripped to shreds, our beards steadily more blood-stained with blackfly bites, and our bodies weary from climbing over all the deadfall and trudging through thickets. Frequently we exhausted ourselves climbing steep, forested hills that ran across our path. The unseasonably hot weather further drained our energy.

"Well," I said, panting, "I think we should make a detour to our left, to find the main stream again and refill our water bottles. Since it looks like we're still several hours at least from reaching the mountains."

"Good idea," said Zach.

We cut to our left, keeping one eye on the sun to guide us, until we scrambled over a few steep hills and found our way back to the main stream. It was surprisingly large and tranquil where we came upon it, making us wonder whether it might be better to simply follow it to the mountains. Although it would make navigating easier, we soon abandoned this idea, as its banks were steep and intersected with many ravines, each smothered in alder thickets and innumerable raspberry thorns. We had to veer off back inland, away from the stream, where the vegetation wasn't as thick.

"How does this compare to your triathlon races?" I asked Zach.

"Well, normally during a triathlon I don't have thorns jabbing into me, and branches smacking me in the face, and logs smashing my shins, and blackflies and mosquitoes eating me alive, or a heavy backpack on and no solid ground under my feet," replied Zach. "But other than that, it's pretty similar."

Eventually we reached a sort of forested plateau where the spruce woods were slightly less dense. Here shafts of sunlight streamed through the canopy, revealing everywhere an unbroken carpet of green moss. Scattered across the moss grew red mushrooms—rosy russulas, which are edible. The ancient, scaly black spruces were mostly free of branches here, aside from the tufts of needles at their crowns. If ever I felt as if I'd strayed into some enchanted woods, it was this quiet, undisturbed spot far from any human place. We pushed forward quietly, weaving between the spruces, sinking with each step into the soft moss.

Ahead came a flash of movement among the trees. It was a woodpecker, which landed on a decayed spruce. The bird began to peck vigorously away; the sound of its drumming filled the woods, echoing in all directions. We crept a bit closer and identified it as a black-backed woodpecker. Unlike most northern woodpeckers, these hardy birds don't migrate and instead live in Canada's subarctic forests year-round, even in the depths of winter.

Beyond, the forest thinned even more, the spruces and tamaracks growing scragglier. A few more exhausted steps and we emerged from the woods into a wide-open vista. It was a muskeg or bog, which stretched onward for at least half a kilometre. The open expanse meant that we finally had an unobstructed view, and all of sudden we could see in detail the splendour of the Mealy Mountains, which stood cloaked in a mantle of dark green and ran in rolling waves along the horizon. The mind reeled at the possibilities for exploration in such vast and wild mountains.

But first we had to get there. We were both in agreement that we'd much rather take our chances traversing the bog than trying to claw through dense forest. So we set off across the open muskeg, staying out of the centre, which looked to be the swampiest. Luckily we were able to walk over the soggy ground without much trouble; it felt like stepping on wet cushions, with a plethora of lichens and moss absorbing our every step.

In the bog were pitcher plants with beautiful bright-coloured flowers, a sort of northern Venus flytrap that eats unsuspecting insects and even frogs. Its prey are lured into the plant's big pitcher, from which they're unable to escape. Inside the pitcher is a sticky liquid containing digestive enzymes that gradually allow the plant to eat its hapless victims. Other characteristic wetland species were here as well: bog rosemary, cotton grasses, and Labrador tea, an aromatic shrub with glossy dark green leaves that were traditionally dried to make tea. I often made Labrador tea on my journeys, and I'd learned that it was wise not to confuse it with bog rosemary, which is a poisonous look alike. Besides these plants were many dwarf tamaracks, tiny but ancient trees that specialize in growing on wet soils. But we couldn't pause to admire them very closely, as intense clouds of blackflies and mosquitoes drove us on.

When we reached the end of the muskeg, we headed back into the shadowy forest. The ground was as uneven as ever, and we found that with all the branches, deadfall, and other obstructions, our bootlaces frequently came undone. Just as I was bending down to retie mine yet again, I noticed fresh bear tracks leading in the same direction we were headed. I pointed them out to Zach.

"Those are huge," he said, bending in to take a look.

"Biggest we've seen so far," I concurred.

"The claws seem bigger on these tracks than on the other ones we've seen," noticed Zach.

"Yes they do," I agreed. "Anyway, we better get a move on. We don't want to be stuck in one of these thickets when the sun goes down."

16

IN THE SHADOW
OF THE MOUNTAIN

The camp lies far away;
We must cross the haunted valley
Before the close of day.
—C.D. Shanly, "The Walker of the Snow," 1859

AFTER ANOTHER KILOMETRE of difficult hiking, which just about completed the ruin of my pants, the ground began to slope steeply upward. Large boulders and rock outcrops, covered in moss and spruces, loomed up around us. This was an encouraging sign; it meant we had to be getting near to the start of the mountains, although given the impossibly thick woods, we couldn't see them. To our left, hidden somewhere behind spruces, roared the stream; the increase in elevation must have turned it into roaring cataracts. It was getting late, and we started to look about for somewhere to camp.

But there wasn't any level ground in sight; hummocks and hollows were everywhere, such that we'd be lucky to find even two feet of flat space. There was no choice but to push on farther, into the gathering gloom. Our legs burned as we staggered uphill, following, though we could not see it, the sound of the stream crashing over boulders and rocks. We'd evidently reached the start of the cleft in the mountains where the stream tumbled down, and now, theoretically, if we kept following this route, we'd make it up into the mountains.

At last, almost delirious from dehydration and blackfly bites, we could go on no further and stumbled into an area of shrubby, mossy forest that was slightly less dense. Here, through the trees, we could make out the shape of a high mountain immediately to the west of us. We'd managed to reach its lower slopes, which formed one half of the valley or cleft between the mountains. For better or worse, this lonely spot in the shadows of the mountains would have to do. I collapsed in exhausted delirium on the soft moss while the bugs swarmed us.

All around us the spruces and tamaracks had been strangely contorted by the mountain gales. Unthinkingly, almost mechanically, I groped along the mossy ground, searching for any wild berries to restore my energy. Fortunately, there were some blueberries, lingonberries, and crowberries. I couldn't resist removing my mesh bug net to eat them, even though it meant getting attacked full in the face by blackflies and mosquitoes.

Zach meanwhile had slouched against a moss-covered boulder. It was then that I noticed his knife was missing from the sheath on his belt.

"Your knife is gone," I said.

"What?" Zach glanced at his belt. "Shoot, it must have fallen out somewhere in the thickets as we were climbing over logs."

"A few thousand years from now it'll make an interesting discovery for some archaeologist," I said.

"Damn, now I don't have a weapon."

"You still have your vampire stake," I said, pointing to the broken paddle he'd converted to a walking stick.

"That'll have to do."

I staggered back to my feet to unpack my backpack and set up my tent. As I did so, I reached for my bug net, which I'd left on the ground beside me. Only it wasn't there. I looked around: there wasn't any sign of it. I was certain I'd put it down right beside me. How could it have just vanished? In disbelief I looked around again. I could feel my mind starting to stray to irrational places, almost believing that some unseen presence had scooped it up. Perhaps these gnomes or elves or whatever they were had also taken Zach's knife. But the rational side of my brain dismissed this as delusion brought on by dehydration and exhaustion. I told myself that I was just tired. I'd find the bug net in the morning when I was better rested.

Zach had wandered off to gather some firewood. I hurried after him to build the smokiest fire we could, as the smoke would help drive off the clouds of bugs. We made our fire on top of a partly flat boulder, about the size of a car. Even with a smoky fire, the blackflies were relentless; we had to crouch right near the blaze to keep them off us.

"What shall we do for water?" asked Zach.

"Hmm . . ."

We wandered through the woods over to the sound of the stream to take a look. It was as we'd suspected: a wild cataract at the bottom of a deep gully, about a hundred feet below us. The sides were very steep, and climbing all the way down to fill the cooking pot and water bottles in our already exhausted state would be risky. Either one of us might slip and smash our head off a rock, which didn't seem particularly desirable just now.

"I think," I said, "we can probably find some other source of water up here, and avoid climbing down there. There's almost always some stagnant pool in these subarctic woods, in my experience."

We set off into the crooked, moss-draped tamaracks and spruces to search for a little pool. Sure enough, in the shadows of some bigger spruces and moss-covered boulders, we came upon a tiny, shallow pond. Our cooking pot we filled here, then returned to our camp.

Zach and I sat by the flickering fire waiting for our meals to cook. We'd have to forego drinking much water, since we were reluctant to drink too much from the pond. The water-purifier we'd left behind at our base camp to lighten our loads, and since we'd only purified one pot's worth of water by boiling it, we'd have to ration it. We both felt light-headed from dehydration and hundreds of blackfly bites, which probably wasn't helped by breathing in campfire smoke.

The sun had nearly sunk below the western mountain peaks, leaving us in lengthening shadow. With the sun disappearing, the temperature had begun to plunge, bringing a welcome relief from the bugs, which can't operate in temperatures much below twelve degrees Celsius. I leaned against the mossy rock outcrop and stretched my feet out toward the fire, while Zach had his back against a balsam fir that grew through a cleft in the rocks. The rock was Precambrian, ancient almost beyond human conception, dating back more than nine hundred million years to a time when Earth was a barren wasteland, with just the first hints of multicellular life forms beginning to emerge.

The hypnotic roar of the stream cascading unseen nearby lulled us into a sort of trance, or spell, deepened by our sheer exhaustion from the intense, punishing effort required to reach this inaccessible place—when travelling one mile had felt more like twenty given all the deadfall, thorns, uneven ground, and blackflies. The wafting smoke from our fire, growing shadows, and thick, dark green moss that smothered everything contributed to the sense we were in a kind of waking dream. Glancing around us at the ancient trees and even more ancient rocks, and seeing the vague outlines of the surrounding mountains through the spruces, it felt as if we were in some forgotten land of myth and legend, the lair of dragons and sorcerers.

"I thought wading through those rapids yesterday was hard. But after today, I'm reconsidering my definition of hard," said Zach, as he mixed up his freeze-dried mac and cheese with a fork.

"We'll be in rags by the time this is over," I said.

The fire burned low, wreaths of smoke rising and drifting above the dark, twisted spruces that encircled us. Just then I thought I heard a faint noise, almost like a whisper, strange and unnatural, echoing apparently from caves higher up the forested slope. It sent a shiver down my spine. But it might have been only the distant sound of the mountain stream tumbling over rocks.

"Did you hear something?" I asked.

Zach paused from eating and listened. The wind whispered softly through the surrounding spruces. He shook his head.

"Probably just the wind," I concluded.

"Well either that or a demon beast," said Zach.

A blast of cold air suddenly came down the mountainside, causing the spruces around us to creak and moan. I shivered in the cold. "I don't know about you, but lately I can't seem to get the image of a grinning, fanged creature with dark fur and a white mane stalking through the woods out of my mind."

"That's what you get from reading all those old accounts at night in your tent," said Zach.

I nodded. "Maybe, but I've learned a lot of useful things from them."

"I'll admit," said Zach, "it's creepy to think of something like that sneaking up to our tents in the darkness to smash us over the head."

"To take us back to their lair to eat later," I mused. In spite of ourselves, our conversations seemed to frequently circle back to the existence of the mystery creature.

"Of course, in a place like Labrador it's easy for the mind to make irrational fears seem plausible," added Zach, casting a glance beyond the fire circle at the darkened spruces, their claw-like branches silhouetted against the ancient boulders. By now the moon was rising, half concealed by drifting clouds.

When we'd finished our meals and the fire had died, we didn't linger, but crept back to our tents in the moonlight. Zach disappeared into his with the broken paddle, while I slipped off my hiking boots, which were wet from walking across the bog, and left them outside my tent. Then I crawled inside, leaving the tent's rain fly unzipped to let a little moonlight spill in and give me enough faint light to arrange my things.

The ground wasn't very comfortable; there were depressions at either end of my tent as well as rocks and roots running underneath and jabbing me in the back. But I rolled up my jacket and extra clothing, and used that to fill in one of the depressions as best I could for my head to rest there. I had a tiny bit of water left over in my thermos from what we'd boiled, and I now drained the last of it.

Just as I was putting my water bottle down, I heard something approach from outside. It sounded big, with brush moving and twigs snapping. Instinctively I yelled in a deep voice and grabbed the bear spray. When in the past I'd had bears approach my tent, yelling like that was often enough to make them freeze, giving me time to get to my feet. Quickly I unzipped my tent and poked my head out, bear spray in hand and ready to use.

"What is it?" Zach's voice came from inside his tent.

I glanced around at the clawing spruces and gnarled, twisted firs, contorted in weird shapes by the fierce winds.

"I thought I heard a bear," I said.

Zach unzipped his tent and looked out. It was difficult to differentiate shapes in the gloom of the moonlight. We waited for a few tense minutes, darting glances every which way. Nothing further was to be heard. A few moments more and we turned back inside our tents.

I lay back down in my sleeping bag, but kept my knife and the bear spray handy. There was definitely something about this place that made me uneasy.

17

NIGHT TERRORS

They told us that two or three families of Natives
had been devoured by large unknown animals . . .
—Father Le Jeune, *Jesuit Relations*, 1633

ROLLING OVER IN MY SLEEP, a root poking into my back woke me up. I glanced at my watch: it was just after midnight. My sleep had been restless and fitful; I couldn't get comfortable on the sloped, uneven ground, and kept getting an eerie feeling that something lurked outside in the darkness. When I did drift off, I'd been having strange, feverish dreams, with odd forest sounds disturbing my sleep.

At intervals came creaking, moaning noises from the crooked spruces swaying in the wind—at least I assumed it was the spruces. I sat up and glanced out my tent: in the silver moonlight the black spruces and firs had taken on a ghostly appearance, their branches draped in old man's beard, a type of hanging lichen. It was a windy night, and with the sound of the wind gusting down the mountain mingled with the creaking trees and the roaring of the river, making out distinct sounds was

"Zach led the way this time, grabbing the canoe and plunging back down into the frigid river. He powered up the alder-lined bank, grabbing with his right hand at the branches, and with his left dragging the canoe up the rapids."

Zach wading up more rocky rapids.

"The foliage had become so dense that even though Zach and I were only a few feet apart, in places we could barely see each other." Zach is the small, blue blur to my right, hidden in the alders.

Bushwhacking on foot to the mountains.

"A few more exhausted steps and we emerged from the woods into a wide-open vista. It was a muskeg or bog, which stretched onward for at least half a kilometre. The open expanse meant that we finally had an unobstructed view, and all of sudden we could see in detail the splendour of the Mealy Mountains..."

A large and fresh bear track, with claw marks clearly defined at the top of the print.

Gaining elevation as we head into the mountains.

"Clawing my way over a fallen spruce, I suddenly paused midway through at the sight of something that sent a shiver down my spine—a cave entrance."

Climbing the mountain.

"Fortunately, we found another small cleft in the rocks filled with cold water, where we were able to replenish our bottles."

My tent set up on the mountain plateau, near the thickets of dwarf spruce and the giant square-shaped boulder. Zach's sheltered nook is out of the frame.

"The whole impression felt as if we were looking at some prehistoric landscape, elemental and as yet undisturbed by the modern world, a wilderness of mystery and legend."

Crawling into a mountain cave.

". . . we made the best of our situation, and camped in the middle of open muskeg, where the annoyance of the blood-sucking insects was at least compensated for by the magnificent view of the mountains behind us. They stood dark and mysterious-looking . . ."

"They'd been only a few feet in front of the lens—*giant pointed tracks like cloven hoofs,* with only two big toes."

difficult. Instead they all blurred together into a kind of unnerving half-whispering moan.

I shivered in the cold and pulled the sleeping bag tighter around me. My mind was still restless, so I decided to give up on sleeping and do some research instead. I switched on my flashlight. It flickered for a moment then went out. I shook it until the light revived. It was cold; I could see my breath in my tent. With the faint light, I sorted through my photocopies. I'd left most of them behind in the barrel, packing only a few for our trek. Flipping through the pages, eventually I settled on some copies I'd made of Indigenous elders' stories pertaining to the Mealy Mountains. These I figured might prove useful. The stories had been told by Pien and Nishet Penashue, elders from Sheshatshiu, a small community on the north shore of Lake Melville. They'd been recorded back in the early 2000s, when the two were in their eighties, by the anthropologist Peter Armitage.

I spread out the pages and flashlight in hand, commenced to read. The Mealy Mountains, according to what the elders said, were inhabited by all kinds of strange, supernatural beings:

Some of these beings such as Meminteu and Atshen were extremely dangerous cannibals. Others like Uapanatsheu and Memekueshu were relatively harmless as long as they were left alone and treated with respect. The Uapanatsheu . . . were sneaking creatures that normally could not be seen, but whose presence was felt when they stole from traps and camps and threw stones and twigs at tents.

"Hmm," I muttered to myself, "maybe that's what stole my bug net?" As I lay pondering this I suddenly heard something brush against the tent. I reached for my knife. Perhaps it was only my imagination? A second later I heard the noise again; *something* was rubbing against the tent's outer rain fly, only three feet away. Silently I rose to my knees, and clutching the knife, slowly unzipped the door, my heart pounding.

In the moonlight I couldn't see anything immediately outside. I found my flashlight and shone the beam into the woods. There didn't appear to be anything; just the dead trees and gloomy spruces and tamaracks all around us. I crept outside onto the soft moss that muffled my footsteps, looking about. My flashlight flickered again, then died.

Shivering, I shook the light. This time it didn't revive. I blinked, trying to adjust to the dark and make out what I could in the moonlight. I thought I heard something whisper nearby; just the wind, I told myself. Then, stepping around to the far side of my tent, in the faint gloom I saw dimly what had made the noise: the branches of a tamarack sapling had been brushing against my tent. I let out a sigh of relief, then tucked back inside and zipped up my tent's screen door.

After digging some fresh batteries out of my backpack, I resumed reading: "The Memekueshu were subterranean people who lived in rocky places and behind cliff faces." There were certainly a number of spots around here matching that description. Apparently, a group of travellers in the mountains had once come across one of these beings, who had chased them: "This Memekueshu was really ugly, having a two-dimensional face, with his eyes on one side." This made me wonder about all the caves in the area; it occurred to me there must be hundreds of them hidden away in these mountains. Who knew what might be found in them? After all, only within the last few years had scientists discovered new and previously unsuspected species in caves elsewhere in the world.

Once more I could hear the wind gusting, the ancient trees moaning. It made me feel a little uneasy. To try to put my mind at ease I kept reading, which in retrospect might not have been the best idea. The Mealy Mountains, it turned out, were traditionally regarded as a kind of haunted range—rather like Europe's Carpathian Mountains, with their dark legends of vampires and werewolves. Many local place names reflected these beliefs; among the names mentioned by the elders were *Manitupeuk(u)* ("Evil Creature Mountain Lake"), *Memekueshunipi* ("Cave Creature Lake"), and *Uapanatsheu-nipi* ("Sneaking Creature Lake").

I switched off the flashlight and lay back in my sleeping bag, staring up at the tent ceiling in the faint moonlight. Why did people traditionally believe malevolent creatures lived in the mountains? Might these folk beliefs have carried a sort of parable intended to keep unwary travellers from straying into places where bad things could happen? Rock slides, loose boulders, bears, avalanches, dangerous wind gusts, and lightning strikes were all very real dangers in the mountains after all, and good reason to stay out of them.

It reminded me very much of traditional Scandinavian lore, which similarly held that the mountains and deep woods were home to supernatural creatures, especially trolls. In Scandinavian lore, trolls typically came in two forms: big, clumsy, ill-tempered and potentially cannibalistic ogres, which seemed rather like windigos, as well as smaller, less overtly violent but still potentially dangerous ones that sometimes hid things and played tricks on humans, which seemed like the sneaking creatures mentioned by the elders as living in the Mealys. Then again, most of these mountain-dwelling creatures didn't seem particularly similar to the descriptions of the Traverspine beast. However, one that might align more closely with it was the Atshen or Atchen, which the elders had said were extremely dangerous creatures that stalked and ate humans (especially dumb ones who were foolish enough to wander into remote parts of the Mealy Mountains).

I recognized the name Atchen from some of my earlier reading. Back in the 1850s, the explorer Henry Youle Hind had called it "the terror and bugbear" of Labrador. Hind said that, whenever its tracks were discovered, the terror they sparked would last for months. The American anthropologist Frank G. Speck, who'd travelled to Labrador to study the Naskapi culture in the 1930s, had also heard whispered tales of the Atchen. Speck referred to it as a "fearsome creature" and, curiously, said that it paralleled the belief among the French Canadian inhabitants of Labrador and northern Quebec in the *loup-garou*—the French name for werewolf.

This was very interesting, given that the Michelin family who lived at Traverspine were of mostly French Canadian descent. I wondered whether the connection between this dreaded "Atchen" and the trappers' and lumberjacks' corresponding belief in the loup-garou might be related to the Traverspine beast. After all, in the folklore of French Canada, which stretches back to the earliest days of New France, there are many traditions about loup-garous or werewolves prowling the wilderness. Long after werewolf beliefs had died out in the Quebec countryside, perhaps they'd continued to survive in the remote and isolated reaches of Labrador? Lonely little places like Traverspine, cut off from the outside world? Of course, it wasn't that I believed in werewolves, or for that matter Atchens, but if the local settlers a century ago had, it might prove a clue to unravelling the mystery.

Jacques Cartier had said in the 1500s that he thought Labrador, with its desolate mountains, was the land "God gave to Cain." When the first hardy French settlers had begun to hack a living out of the wilderness in Canada, they too had held in dread the northern spruce-cloaked mountains that hemmed in their settlements. They avoided Labrador and settled on the southern end of the range along the St. Lawrence coast. Around these French settlers' hearths there were whispers about strange, nameless horrors lurking in the distant mountains.

Paul Le Jeune, an early Jesuit missionary, reported an alarming incident that occurred at the foot of the mountains in November 1633. He wrote that "large unknown animals" had "devoured" entire families, which probably wasn't very encouraging to the newly arrived settlers. Le Jeune's testimony translated into English reads:

On the eighth, Manitougache, surnamed la Nasse, and all his family, consisting of two or three households, came and

> encamped near our house. They told us that two or three fam-
> ilies of Natives had been devoured by large unknown animals,
> which they believed were Devils; and that the Montagnaits,
> fearing them, did not wish to go hunting in the neighbour-
> hood of Cape de Tourmente and Tadoussac, these monsters
> having appeared in that neighbourhood . . .

The French settlers were not alone in their dread: the nomadic
Algonquian nations that lived in the area held similar beliefs
that the north woods and mountains were the hunting grounds
of a terrifying creature. Le Jeune, who'd learned the local tribal
dialect, noted that the word for this "demon" was "Atchen"—
the very same word that four hundred years later the elders in
Labrador had used to describe the fearsome creature that supposedly lived in the Mealy Mountains. Le Jeune had translated
Atchen as meaning "a sort of werewolf."

Another French Jesuit, Father Fabvre, heard a different
name for the creatures—*windigo*. But he too understood it as
signifying something akin to what the French called loup-garou
or in English *werewolf*. The anthropologist Frank Speck had
concluded that the Atchen and the windigo were separate but
related creatures, which were often confused. The Atchen seems
to have been found farther north, in Labrador especially, while
the windigo were distributed all across the subarctic forests. But
both were said to be large, hideous monsters that lurked in the
mountains and hungered for human prey.

Although much has been made of the cultural gulf separating Indigenous nations from European colonists, on this subject

at least, the French and Algonquians were in agreement. Europe in the sixteenth and seventeenth centuries was very different from today. It was still recovering from the ravages of the Black Death, which had killed nearly half the continent's population. Much of Europe remained a wilderness of dark forests, mountains, bogs, and inaccessible hills. The vast majority of the population was rural—few of the French settlers had ever seen a city, let alone lived in one. Wolves and bears prowled about in great numbers, and belief in magic, the supernatural, and witchcraft was commonplace. As a result, most French settlers in Canada didn't ridicule their Algonquian neighbours' belief in Atchens or windigos. On the contrary, they took such tales seriously, interpreting them as similar to their own beliefs in werewolves and vampires. Not until the European Enlightenment of the eighteenth century—when science expanded by leaps and bounds—did such beliefs begin to fall out of favour.

Further tales of werewolves prowling the Quebec countryside emerged periodically, including in the 1760s when a local newspaper, the *Gazette de Québec*, reported:

By accounts from St. Rock, near Cap Mouraska, we learn, that there is a werewolf wandering about that Neighbourhood, in the Form of a Beggar ... It is said that this Animal came, by the Assistance of his two hind Legs, to Quebec the 17th of last Month, and set out from hence the 18th following ... This Beast is said to be as dangerous as that which appear'd last Year in the Country of Gevaudan [in France]; wherefore it is recommended to the Public to be as cautious of him as it would be of a ravenous Wolf.

The newspaper's mention of "Gevaudan" was a reference to one of the most notorious "werewolf" incidents ever to occur in France. Between 1764 and 1765 in France's mountainous Gévaudan region, terror reigned as over a hundred shepherds and peasants were killed, many with their throats ripped out and their bodies partly eaten. Rumours spread that a werewolf was on the prowl; at night families barred their doors and slept with axes, scythes, and other weapons. The panic spread across the countryside, prompting the French king to respond by dispatching huntsmen to track and slay the creatures responsible. But the killings continued unabated, until finally, in the fall of 1765, the King's Gun-Bearer, an experienced hunter named François Antoine, succeeded in tracking down and killing the dreaded "Beast of Gévaudan." The "monster" turned out to be an enormous male wolf, measuring almost six feet long and weighing nearly a hundred and forty pounds. Officials concluded that the widespread killings had been the work of both this monster wolf and other wolves in its pack, rather than anything supernatural—although many villagers continued to insist long afterward that a shape-shifting werewolf had been the real culprit.

Meanwhile back in Quebec, in December 1767—a year after the first reports surfaced of a werewolf on the loose in the Canadian countryside—wild rumours circulated that the same werewolf had been spotted again. It was reported that the werewolf, "which has roamed through this Province for several Years,

and done great Destruction ... has received several considerable Attacks." The newspaper reported that the local Canadian
settlers had succeeded in tracking the beast and setting their
hunting dogs upon it. However, to their great "misfortune," the
paper informed readers that, "this Beast is not entirely destroyed,
but begins again to shew itself, more furious than ever, and makes
terrible Hovock [havoc] wherever it goes." The report concluded
with a warning for readers to "beware" of this "malicious Beast,
and take good care of falling into its Claws."

It is easy to suppose that the basis for many of these monster
beliefs were actual animal attacks—something that is relatively
uncommon in our modern world, which has pushed back the
wilderness in all directions and laid waste to wildlife popula-
tions, but was a grim fact of life for many earlier societies. Indeed,
there's little doubt that wolves really did kill large numbers
of people across Europe's wild hinterlands for centuries. New
research has revealed that what had once been regarded as little
more than fairy tales to frighten children—ravenous wolves that
routinely killed and ate humans—were, in reality, common. One
recent study found that in France alone, wolves were responsible
for hundreds of attacks on humans every year, from the Middle
Ages right through the eighteenth century—overlapping with
the period of French settlement in Canada. This seems to have
been driven partly by the overhunting of deer, which deprived
wolves of their normal prey, although it also seems that wolves
preyed on humans even when other food sources were available. (After all, humans, especially children, are quite slow and
tender compared to deer.) These wolf attacks on humans were

particularly common before the widespread introduction of firearms. Neither poor French shepherds nor Algonquian hunters
normally had guns, making both vulnerable to attacks by bears
and wolves.

Many of these incidents were likely embellished into terrifying supernatural attacks, be it werewolves or windigos, or the
in case of Labrador, the monstrous Atchen. Eventually, through
the fur trade and intermarriage, werewolf tales eventually mixed
with those of the Atchen. Speck, the anthropologist, had said as
much when he found that the Naskapi and Montagnais belief
in the Atchen corresponded with their neighbouring French
Canadian lumberjacks' and trappers' werewolf beliefs. But if
belief in the loup-garou had originally been inspired by actual
wolf attacks, what had originally inspired belief in the Atchen?
Perhaps it had been based on bear attacks?

Bear attacks were not, of course, unknown in Labrador.
As the explorer Henry Youle Hind noted in the 1850s, "The
bears of Labrador are large and formidable, and when hungry
very ferocious. They have been known to attack and kill Indians
during the night-time when sleeping under their canoes."
Hind related that one of his guides named Louis told him that
he "knew a Canadian who was swamped with his canoe in a
rapid . . . One month afterwards he found his bones in the bush
a mile from the river." As the guide explained to Hind, "Bear
found body, dragged it into the bush, eat it." It's easy to imagine how, over time, some of these disturbing cases might give
rise to legends like the man-eating Atchen or werewolf—just
imagine deep in some dark forest finding a human skeleton

with the bones crushed and broken apart by a bear so as to suck out the marrow . . .

However, by the end of the nineteenth century, belief in the werewolf had largely died out in rural Quebec. The growth of cities and towns, the clearing of forests, damming of rivers, industrialization, and the widespread introduction of better firearms had tamed the wilds and simultaneously slayed many supernatural fears of monsters lurking there. But the tradition had possibly survived in Labrador among isolated French Canadian lumberjacks and trappers, like the Michelin family at Traverspine. Marcel Michelin was the first Michelin to settle in Labrador. He was a French Canadian from Trois-Rivières who arrived in Labrador in 1834 and settled near the Kenemich River, before later relocating to the Traverspine River. As such, he carried with him traditions of the dreaded loup-garou that went back centuries.

There was certainly something about the vastness of Labrador and its extensive uninhabited areas that seems to have lent itself to monster legends. In the early twentieth century, Frank Speck, who'd spent years tramping the wilds of Labrador, noted what he called, "the opportunity for the play of fear-inspired imagination offered by these immense solitudes." Although compared to how vast the territory was, with its ancient mountains and primeval forests, Speck actually felt that "the number of apparitions inhabiting the forests and barrens is rather small." But lying inside my tent in the dark miles from anywhere, tallying up all the different monsters and supernatural creatures mentioned by the elders, I wasn't so sure I agreed with Speck on that point. In any case, it was easy to see how Labrador—where the distance between trading posts might be many hundreds of miles—left plenty of room to imagine terrifying creatures like Atchens and werewolves lurking in the shadows just beyond the glow of the campfire.

On the other hand, the eyewitness descriptions of the Traverspine creatures didn't sound like something based on a wolf or a bear. Perhaps they'd been inspired by encounters with some other animal? Or maybe something else altogether? Eventually, with visions of werewolves and Atchens and other nameless terrors on my mind, I finally shut my eyes and fell asleep.

18

TRACKING THE UNKNOWN

He comes,—he comes,—the Frost Spirit comes! from the frozen Labrador,
From the icy bridge of the Northern seas, which the white bear wanders o'er
—John Greenleaf Whittier, "The Frost Spirit," 1850

THE MORNING DAWNED grey and wet. I awoke groggy and disoriented after a mostly sleepless night, in which I'd had fitful dreams and kept waking every hour. I was eager to be out of this eerie valley and on our way into the open country above the treeline.

Shivering in my tent, I decided to keep my warm base layer on underneath my outer clothing for the day. Then I pulled on my black rain jacket, put on my torn gloves, donned my faded Tilley hat, and crawled out of the tent without the benefit of any bug net. The forest was wet and sodden, which seemed to make the green moss that smothered everything even more vivid and fairy tale–like. A light rain was falling.

"Are you awake?" I asked, looking at Zach's tent.

"No," came Zach's voice from within.

"Oh," I said. "How did you sleep?"

"Not well . . . the ground wasn't very comfortable and I kept hearing strange noises. How about you?"

"The same."

"I'm feeling dehydrated. I think our first priority should be to fetch water," said Zach.

"Good idea. I'm feeling pretty light-headed myself," I said.

We left our tents up and our backpacks beside them, but took our water bottles and thermoses and headed through the woods to the edge of the narrow ravine where the mountain stream cascaded a hundred feet below. We hadn't wanted to drink untreated water from the stagnant pool in the forest, particularly since it was plain that animals like bears and moose and who knew what else walked through it. But there was little to fear from drinking untreated water from the mountain stream—the only question was getting down to it. A rope would have been handy, but we didn't have one with us. We'd have to manage the climb without it.

Fortunately the gully was thickly wooded, and we could use the spruces and firs to lower ourselves down the sides. As we neared the bottom, the incline became steeper and slicker, and we had to choose our steps with care to avoid slipping on the wet moss. In the stream were giant boulders; we cautiously climbed out onto these to fill our bottles. The water felt cold as ice as it plunged and cascaded over numerous rocks and boulders, creating small whirlpools and eddies.

"I will never taste water better than that as long as I live," said Zach.

He filled his bottle and drank it completely, and then refilled it a second time. I too drank as much as I could, since we didn't know when we'd be able to find water again. Our plan was to climb the mountain we'd camped at the base of. It seemed to be the highest point among the peaks we'd seen, and if we could reach the top, or near to it, we'd plan to spend the night there and explore any caves in the area.

But to scale the mountain would require ample drinking water. So after refreshing ourselves from the stream, we filled our thermoses with cold water in addition to our water bottles. This gave us about two litres each, which would have to last us until we could find a spring or some other water source higher up the mountain.

We wasted little time returning to our camp, packing up our tents and gear, and strapping on our backpacks. There was still no sign of my bug net, and I resigned myself to accepting that it had vanished, or else blended in so well with the Labrador tea shrubs and ferns that I'd never find it. In any case, there wasn't time to mourn its loss: we set off through the spruces. A dismal cloud of blackflies and mosquitoes followed us as we went, but at least the rain had ceased.

Zach carried the snapped-off paddle as a walking stick, and I had the can of bear spray in the outer mesh pocket of my backpack. The ground sloped steeply upward, but was still very mossy and soft. Only a few minutes from our camp the forest became as thick as it was the day before, and we were again climbing over deadfall, or else crawling under it, and weaving between spruces. This time around, we'd taken the precaution of taping up our hiking boots, so that the laces didn't come undone in thickets. This worked like a charm and saved us from constantly retying our boots, as had been the case the day before.

The forest on these lower mountain slopes was composed of balsam fir and spruce, but also white birch and even a few mountain ashes, as well as alder thickets wherever there seemed to be some greater dampness. The trees were mostly small and densely packed, while cloaking the ground beneath them were thick sphagnum moss, large ferns, Labrador tea, blueberries, mushrooms of various kinds, and an abundance of red bunchberries. Some of the leaves on the birches and alders had begun to fade to yellow with the first hints of fall, but others were still green.

Tunnelling through a thicket, battling branches and spiderwebs every which way, I suddenly came upon bear tracks. They looked fresh, and a few strides ahead I could see a huge pile of unmistakably fresh bear excrement.

"Look at this," I said to Zach, pointing out the bear's droppings. The steaming pile was really large, uncomfortably so, and fresh-looking.

Zach staggered up through the thick brush behind me to take a look. "It would be interesting to see just how big these bears are," he said, studying the specimen.

"Their droppings seem larger than the ones I see in Ontario from black bears," I replied.

"I guess it's September, so the bears are eating more and putting on weight for the winter," mused Zach.

"That's true," I said. Then a thought crossed my mind. "Do you think you could take a bear in a fight?"

"With a weapon?"

"No, with your hands. Like using one of your mixed martial arts moves?"

"I don't think so."

"Couldn't you put it in some kind of headlock or arm-bar or something?"

"Bears are freakishly strong, and I think it would just claw the hell out of me if I tried anything," replied Zach thoughtfully.

"Oh . . . Well, I suppose we should get a move on."

Zach nodded and we pressed forward through the thicket and up the increasingly steep slope. As we gained elevation a view opened up behind us of the mountains framing the valley. Immediately across from us loomed another steep, heavily wooded mountain, one with multiple rocky peaks that rose one after another like the humps on some prehistoric monster. To the northwest of this mountain, the land fell abruptly away to the lowlands of bogs and dense woods that we'd crossed the day before. Above us the sky remained overcast, and a light wind was blowing from the north.

We kept hiking; the ground became steadily steeper and big boulders and cliff faces began to appear, forcing us to switchback to get around them. Blackflies dogged us, although they weren't nearly as vicious as they'd been in the swamps. That morning I'd changed into my second pair of hiking pants, my other pair having been literally ripped to shreds by the time we'd made camp. The dead spruces, however, wasted no time in ripping a hole in my new pants.

Clawing my way over a fallen spruce, I suddenly paused midway through at the sight of something that sent a shiver down my spine—a cave entrance. It was tucked between several giant moss-covered boulders, with small balsam firs growing on top of them and all around it. The dark opening into the cave was about three or four feet high.

"Well if I were a Traverspine gorilla, or a demon, I think that'd make a lovely home," said Zach.

"It certainly looks like it," I concurred.

With a bit of nervousness we approached the entrance. It looked promising, with dead leaves and carpets of moss spreading along the ground immediately outside it, and extending into the entrance. But I didn't see any discarded bones lying outside or crushed skulls, such as we figured a demon creature might leave outside its den. Nor was there any sign of tracks leading to or from the cave. After a moment's hesitation, I leaned down and looked inside. It was empty.

"Not even a bear," I said.

"What a shame," agreed Zach.

We continued up the mountainside. Now we were *really* climbing, scrambling along the rocks and ground and using our hands to cautiously pull ourselves up. The vegetation began to change, with juniper bushes appearing on the exposed cliffs, as juniper prefers drier soils than the vegetation we'd seen lower down. There were more caves, too, ranging from hobbit-sized to bear-sized. We investigated several of these, all of which looked very habitable, but none had any sign that we could see of anything living in them aside from spiders. However, the thickets and steep incline, combined with our lack of sleep, meant we didn't have the energy to climb laterally to explore every one of the caves. Some of them had to be left unexamined.

As we neared the crest of the mountain, we were confronted by a big vertical rock wall. It forced us to shimmy to our left, along the cliff face, to find a less precipitous route. Fortunately we spotted a small cleft in the rocks, where some scrubby juniper bushes and little dwarf spruces clung to the cliff. Here we managed to scramble our way up using the bushes, though our heavy backpacks made our balance precarious. A stumble here and we'd careen back down the mountain until the trees stopped our plummet, undoubtedly breaking many bones in the process, which would probably spoil the day.

After a few more feet of difficult scrambling, I pulled myself up to a small windswept plateau, which was above the treeline but still about a hundred metres below the mountain's summit. Zach scrambled up after me. Panting heavily, we sprawled out and rested on the ground. Around us lay ancient lichen-covered boulders and small alpine plants and shrubs; scattered here and there, mostly in sheltered nooks, grew clumps of alpine dwarf spruces. Near where we'd dropped was a plethora of crowberries and lingonberries—tiny little berries that normally flourish on the arctic tundra by growing close to the ground, out of the harsh winds. We feasted happily on these.

"Look at that view," said Zach, munching on some berries.

I stopped my gathering and cast a glance back at where we'd come. We were high enough now that we could see over the valley below; beyond it lay a sea of dark mountains rolling one after another to the grey horizon. Many of them rose to rounded, weathered peaks of barren rock. They looked inconceivably ancient, and indeed they were: we were looking at one of the oldest mountain ranges on earth. They had once risen to immense heights, but over vast eons of time—more than half a billion years—the elements had worn them down to the rounded peaks of today. The clouds were gathered just above their ancient summits, and it seemed as if we'd be in for a stormy night.

"Let's keep going," I said. "We'd better find some sheltered nook or cave or something where we can drop our backpacks at, and then push on without them to the peak."

"We're going to try making it all the way to the summit?" asked Zach.

"Well we came this far, we might as well give it our best shot. It may not be possible, but in any case, I don't think we can climb any higher with these heavy packs throwing us off balance, especially in this wind." Now that we were above the treeline, the wind had become fierce and cold. On the bright side, it meant no more pesky blackflies or mosquitoes.

"Right, well, let's find a spot then," replied Zach.

It was now mid-afternoon, and we pushed on across the windy plateau toward cliff faces and stupendous grey boulders, hoping to find some route that would lead us to the mountain summit. Soon we crossed a second plateau, higher up than the first, where more giant boulders had been arranged haphazardly, as if they were the playthings of the gods. Smaller rocks, some so oddly shaped as to be almost rectangular, lay scattered about the giant boulders. There was no hint at all of previous travellers here, a fact that reinforced the solitude of the place. Having passed these ancient boulders we came to the other side of the plateau, which sloped down into a kind of sheltered nook beneath a cliff face where some dwarf spruces tenaciously clung to the rocks and grew despite the harsh winds.

"This looks about as good a place as any to camp," I said.

"As good as any place on a mountain can be," agreed Zach.

We left our backpacks beside a rock outcrop on the plateau. Among the dwarf spruces there was enough dead wood that we'd be able to make a fire, and we could pitch our tents beside some of the giant boulders to shelter us from the powerful wind gusts. But there wasn't any water that we could see. So we took our half-empty bottles with us, clipped to carabiners on our belts, in the hope of finding some on the way to the top.

Across a gap or gully in the plateau, the rocky summit loomed up in the clouds. The side nearest to us was precipitous; without rope or climbing gear we wouldn't be able to scale it. But it looked possible that if we circled around we'd be able to approach the peak from behind, as it seemed less steep on that side. To get there we pushed through a dense, tightly packed thicket of dwarf spruces no taller than our chests. These thickets felt almost claustrophobic; in spite of myself, I could almost half believe some creature was hidden in them, lurking about unseen. Coming out of this first thicket, we followed along exposed rock shelves until we came to another spruce-filled gully. Zach and I climbed down a cliff face into it and then fought our way across the thicket to some higher cliffs on the other side.

This final cliff, from what we could tell, led directly to the summit. Carefully we scrambled along a crack in it, where a bit of shrubbery allowed us to pull ourselves up. Without backpacks weighing us down, climbing was much easier. But when we reached the clifftop we found the freezing wind was so powerful that it caused us to stagger backwards. It was without doubt the strongest wind I'd ever felt in my life, and if we weren't careful, the gusts could easily knock us off our feet and straight off the mountain.

We staggered into the wind, our clothing flapping wildly against our bodies as we leaned low to maintain our balance. The wind was howling madly, making talking difficult. The rounded summit was covered in exposed rock, small grasses, and in more sheltered spots, lingonberries and crowberries. We pushed forward toward a rocky upthrust, the highest point of all. A few more steps and we'd reached the summit—we were on the highest peak in the immediate area, some eighteen hundred feet above sea level, which felt higher, since our proximity to the sea coast meant that the vertical rise (the distance from the flat ground to the summit) was actually steeper than on some higher mountains.

However, it wasn't possible to stand on the summit for very long with the dangerous winds knocking us around. We took a few photos, but quickly dropped back down to a ledge a few feet below the summit, where we could more easily take in the panoramic view.

Primordial mountains, weathered by eons of storms, ran northeast as far as the eye could see. They were mostly rounded and levelled off, ground down by the weight of untold ages. The plateaus on top were windswept, barren, rocky wastelands, but below the summits were dark green conifer woods. In the foreground we could make out a white blur of innumerable cascades and roaring rapids where the stream ran through the wooded valley. A lone osprey soared over the valley, far below us and out of the wind. Visible in the other direction, immediately to our left, lay the lowlands that stretched away to the coast of Lake Melville. We could see straight across the lake to the mountains on its north shore. The whole impression felt as if we were looking at some prehistoric landscape, elemental and as yet undisturbed by the modern world, a wilderness of mystery and legend.

19

NIGHT ON THE MOUNTAIN

I sought the wild and rugged glen
Where Nature, in her sternest mood,
Far from the busy haunts of men,
Frowned in darksome solitude.
—James Monroe Whitfield, "The Misanthropist," 1853

T HE SUN WAS FADING and the temperature dropping rapidly. Zach and I had to get a move on, as we still had to make it back to our camp, set up our tents, and build a fire before dark. Fortunately, below the summit on the plateau, we'd found a small rock-bound lake or rather pond; it was about fifty feet long and less than half that in width, which afforded us drinking water. Whether it was fed by some underground spring, or if it had been filled up by melted snow or rainwater, we couldn't tell—but its waters were cold and clear, and we drank from them gratefully. Our water bottles, too, we replenished here, so that we'd be able to make tea and cook our freeze-dried meals back at our camp.

That there was a body of water at all on the mountaintop seemed a geographical curiosity, which reminded me of Arthurian legends of enchanted lakes, and I could almost imagine a Viking sword lying at the bottom of it. It also made me think of eastern Ontario's Lake on the Mountain, and the local lore connected with that place proclaiming it a bottomless pit. Perhaps because the sky was overcast, we couldn't see into the depths of the pond to determine how deep it was, which lent it an air of mystery—a kind of magic pool in these spell-bound mountains. Maybe, with any luck, drinking its waters might give us some kind of enlightenment, or at the very least prevent dehydration, which was nearly as well.

Our bottles filled, Zach and I retraced our steps across the plateau, snacking on lingonberries and crowberries as we went, before descending the steep cliff back to the spruce-filled gully. We climbed and scrambled our way across it, then up onto the rocks, and eventually to where we'd left our backpacks, which fortunately hadn't been ripped open by an animal or otherwise disturbed in our absence.

Given the strong winds and difficulty of staking the tents down on the hard rock, we had to select our tent sites with extra care. Zach found a perfect little sheltered nook beneath a gigantic lichen-covered boulder some fifteen feet high. Its vertical sides provided a partial windbreak, while clustered nearby were thickets of alpine dwarf spruce and a few smaller boulders that could double as tables. Immediately beside the giant boulder lay a little open space devoid of trees, perfect for pitching a tent; the only thing growing there were tiny alpine plants a few centimetres high, huddled and spread out close to the ground, exactly as one finds on the arctic tundra. It was a marvellous campsite, and reminded me of some chieftain's lair in the Scottish

Highlands. Alas, there was only room for a single tent, so I contented myself with a much more exposed site beside a rock outcrop several dozen metres away.

With our tents up, we gathered wood and made a cheering fire in Zach's sheltered nook, which was much more inviting than the exposed area next to my tent. We could sit comfortably there—leaning our backs against the giant boulder, sheltered from the wind, warmed by the fire, and with ample amounts of tiny but delicious crowberries and lingonberries within easy reach. It seemed like just about everything someone could want in life. While snacking on berries we waited for the pot to boil, in order to make some tea and freeze-dried vegetable lasagna.

"I was thinking," said Zach, poking at the fire with a stick, "that if there *was* something in that valley, a bear or a Traverspine demon or whatever, it could easily have watched our ascent up the side of the mountain to this spot."

"True."

"And it might be curious if people don't typically venture out this way," mused Zach.

"It might be," I agreed.

Just then the lid of the pot lifted off as the water reached a full boil. I leaned over to take the pot off the fire and pour it into our thermoses for tea.

"And with the wind gusts on this mountain, we'd never hear its approach while we're sleeping," observed Zach.

"No, we certainly wouldn't," I agreed.

"It gives me the creeps."

Sitting on a mountaintop beside a fire, with the smoke curling upward, put me in a reflective mood, and I found myself recalling in my mind some of the occurrences of our journey so far. It did seem odd how in passing through the impenetrable, shadow-filled thickets on our way here, we kept hearing strange noises, and sometimes had an odd feeling of being watched, as well as finding huge tracks . . . but never what had made them. Of course, we'd figured it had to be bears. But here on this wind-swept mountain, one could almost imagine that it was *something* much more alarming, something nameless that had been following us, silently stalking us this whole time. I remembered with a chill the glowing eyes we'd seen in the dark at one of our camps along the river, and the strange sensation when I found my bug net had vanished, and that Zach's belt-knife had also disappeared.

"Do you believe in demons?" I asked on a whim.

Zach pondered the question for a moment. "If I'm in my office in the middle of the day? No. But in the woods in the middle of the night . . . maybe."

I nodded in agreement. The sun was sinking below the horizon, its last dying rays casting a golden light on the huge ancient boulders around us.

"There's another thing that's been bothering me. Do you find it odd that we haven't seen more animals lately?" Zach asked.

"What do you mean?"

"Well, down in that wooded valley, it occurred to me that we didn't hear, let alone see, any animals—not even so much as the chatter of a red squirrel."

"Almost as if there's something in that mountain valley that makes the animals avoid it?" I said.

"Exactly."

"Hmm . . . and we kept hearing strange noises, and encountering huge tracks . . . but not what's making them," I added, giving voice to my earlier thoughts.

"Odd, isn't it?"

"Very odd . . ." I said.

We said nothing further on the matter, and half famished from our exhausting hike through the thickets and our climb up the mountain, we turned our attention to eating our vegetable lasagna. By the time we'd finished and brushed our teeth, the sun had disappeared altogether, leaving us in darkness on the mountain. Zach and I lingered by the fire, tossing in some spruce branches to kindle a reassuring blaze. Our conversation drifted in other directions, and we discussed our future hopes. Zach said that his great ambition was to save up enough money from his day job in insurance to eventually buy part of the family farm and maintain it. My own dream was to one day find a small patch of forest to call my own and preserve it, where I could wander, think, and dream among the trees.

The night felt a little eerie, with the half moon rising while partially concealed in drifting cloud, and the giant boulders silhouetted by the moonlight. In the gloom, they looked almost like some forgotten Stonehenge. Near my tent stood a great square-shaped boulder that seemed precariously perched on the plateau, just before an abrupt drop-off—and yet it must have lain balancing like that since the last Ice Age thousands of years ago, when huge glaciers carved out the land.

When the fire died we said goodnight and headed for our tents. Inside mine I took off my jacket, rolled it up with my extra clothing, and made a pillow to rest on. The ground beneath was solid rock, but on the bright side it was at least level. With the flashlight I made a few notes in my journal and then turned to my photocopies. In spite of it all, I felt that the clues to the Traverspine mystery were close at hand, and that in one of these mountain caves we might find the answer.

Reviewing one of my old sources, I came across an intriguing observation about Labrador's mountains made fifty years ago by the writer R.S. Lambert. Lambert had been recalling the experiences of an anthropologist who'd done field research in the mountains of Labrador in the 1930s. Lambert noted:

> When the anthropologist J.E. Lips was in Labrador ... he visited a cone-shaped mountain rising above Lake Chibougamou, called "Conqueror's Mountain" that no Indian would consent to climb. Spirits and dwarfs were said to dwell there, including "Metchumentu" ... and "Wit'tigo" ... No one would camp on its slopes for fear of being haunted by bad dreams, sleeplessness, or ghosts.

Maybe it was only a coincidence, but it sure seemed a strange one that Zach and I both couldn't sleep much and were tormented by bad dreams when we camped in the mountain valley. And that had been merely on the lower slope; now we were camped high above on the windswept plateau. The rational side of my brain insisted it was just dehydration that had caused our restless sleep and bad dreams; while the irrational side, that, well ... maybe there *was* something to those old legends.

Beside me were the local oral history accounts; I flipped through some of these. There were more stories from elders about weird and bizarre creatures that had been seen long ago in the Mealy Mountains. My eye caught on some curious accounts I hadn't paid much attention to until now. Several of the old-timer trappers recalled how they'd spotted strange, unnatural lights in the Mealys. They described them as resembling shooting stars that lit up the night sky with an unearthly glow. Once an old trapper in the Mealys, after seeing one of these lights flash across the sky, reported feeling a strange presence about his camp. With him was his faithful dog, a reliable animal that was never known to spook easy or bark without good reason. On this night, though, the dog became agitated, growling with its hair on end at something beyond the fire circle. The trapper had never seen his dog so agitated, and felt too that something was watching them. He passed a sleepless night huddled in fear with his dog by the fire, haunted by an unshakable feeling that some unknown creature was lurking nearby.

I decided it was best not to do any further reading, and for once switch off my flashlight and go straight to bed. Sleep proved difficult though; not so much because of the solid rock beneath me, but rather because of the incessant racket made by the wind gusts shaking my tent. Inside the sound was amplified, and was so deafeningly loud that if a whole herd of caribou galloped by I wouldn't have heard them. It felt as if the wind might lift my tent straight off the mountain and carry me away with it, like Dorothy in *The Wizard of Oz*. Finally, sometime around midnight, I decided I had to do something about it.

I crawled out of my tent into the darkness. The stars above were brilliant, as by now most of the clouds had dissipated on the strong wind. In the moonlight, I could see well enough to gather rocks and use them to build a wall along my tent fly. This bit of improvised masonry would act as a windbreak to keep the gusts from sweeping underneath and rumbling the tent all night. As I gathered rocks in the moonlight, it felt a little eerie to be moving about near the huge, oddly shaped boulders, appearing as they did like some ruined Druidic temple. I paused and looked at them and the surrounding dwarf thickets, which were swaying with each wind gust. There was something thrilling and maybe a little frightening about it all, standing on a mountain plateau in the moonlight, with Zach and I the only living souls around for miles.

Another blast of cold air left me shivering. I dove inside my now wind-fortified tent and crawled back into my sleeping bag.

20

DAWN

The oldest and strongest emotion of mankind is fear, and
the oldest and strongest kind of fear is fear of the unknown.
—H.P. Lovecraft, *Supernatural Horror in Literature*, 1927

T HE MORNING DAWNED with cloud-filled skies, but
we relaxed by our fire in the sheltered nook out of the
wind, sipping tea and making notes and absorbing the atmosphere. With the reassurance of daylight, I tried to banish from
my mind all thoughts of otherworldly things, and take a clear,
calm look at the facts. I felt there had to be a rational explanation behind Traverspine, one that had since gotten mixed up
and embellished. Neither a hoax nor purely a hallucination, the
monster, I felt sure, had a basis in something real in the material
world. All we had to do was deconstruct the supernatural elements that had become encrusted around it. I reflected on all my
sources, along with everything I knew of Canada's wild and the
animals that lived in it.

It was then, going over all the records of the Traverspine
beast in my mind and jotting thoughts down, that I had a sort
of epiphany. Maybe it was the mountain air that had cleared

my head, but at any rate, for the first time I felt confident that I knew what had appeared over a century ago at Traverspine, bewildering and terrifying the residents. Or to be more precise, an idea I'd been turning over for some time at the back of my mind had finally ripened.

I'd noticed a pattern in my reading on Labrador—something conspicuous by its absence. Naturally enough for a place where hunting and trapping were of central importance, all the historical sources I'd collected on early twentieth-century Labrador discussed at length the animals hunted and trapped across the territory, including caribou, bears, wolves, foxes, hares, porcupines, mink, muskrat, beaver, martens, weasels, red squirrels, seals, numerous species of waterfowl and other birds, and even lynx. But curiously enough, there was one creature almost never mentioned, in part because few people had ever seen it, even in Labrador. A creature that elsewhere had inspired strange rumours and legends, and that, coincidentally, matched a lot of the descriptions from Traverspine: the uncanny ability to evade baited traps and to alternate from two legs to four, the ripping apart of rotten logs with great strength, the boldness, the grinning face, and the white ruff or mane. Namely, a wolverine.

Could a wolverine have been the Traverspine beast? Pound for pound, wolverines are one of the hardiest and fiercest creatures in the northern wilderness, capable of killing prey much larger than themselves. They can stalk and kill adult caribou and elk, and even young moose. Their reputation for fearlessness is the stuff of legend, and they possess an almost supernatural toughness, including the ability to chew through their own leg if captured in a steel trap, enabling them to escape and survive with only three legs. They are cunning and clever, capable of eluding even the best hunters and driving wolves from their fresh kills. They'll break into cabins not only to steal food but also to utterly destroy any other items—only to vanish afterward like a ghost. The males weigh up to fifty pounds, although exceptionally large ones may get up to seventy pounds, with huge, impressive jaws. Visually their most striking attribute is their dark fur with a white stripe or ruff across it—the very thing that the eye-witnesses said the Traverspine beast had.

Partly what makes wolverines so rare is that they're solitary creatures, ranging over mind-bogglingly vast territories spanning thousands of kilometres. In a whole lifetime spent in northern forests, a person might never so much as glimpse one—though they might find evidence of one, making them seem like a kind of phantom beast whose presence is felt but never seen. This is reflected in some of the traditional names among trappers for wolverines: historically, they were called "devil beasts" or "devil bears," "mountain devils," "Indian devils," "demon beasts," "skunk bears," and in French, *carcajous*, derived from an Algonquian word meaning "evil spirit." All these names hint at the elusive, phantom-like nature of wolverines, and their uncanny ability to avoid detection. This appeared to be the case with the historical sources from early twentieth-century Labrador, most of which never mentioned wolverines at all.

Even today wolverines remain mysterious. While it might be assumed that nowadays, given satellite tracking, motion-activated trail cameras, helicopters, and other aircraft, scientists would have a very good understanding of the wolverine's range, this isn't the case. Wolverines are so rare and adept at remaining out of sight that they've continued to evade even modern attempts to unravel their secrets. Even a question as simple as where they live is still not entirely known. As far as the wolverine's range in Canada goes, a big question mark looms over Labrador and northern Quebec. As the organization Nature Canada reports, "Today, the eastern population of Wolverines is one of the most misunderstood and least known of Canada's wild animals." Scientists haven't been able to confirm whether wolverines exist here at all. The last wolverine known to have been caught in a trap in Quebec was over forty years ago in 1978, and in Labrador there hasn't been a record of one in over sixty years. This has led many wildlife biologists to conclude that wolverines are extinct in Labrador, although others think there are still some out there, hidden away in remote mountains and woods seldom visited by humans.

Be that as it may, for our purposes of investigating the Traverspine mystery, the crucial fact is that by Merrick's time wolverines were extremely rare in Labrador, if not almost extinct. In other words, few people had any familiarity with them—making them ideal candidates for monster legends to develop around. Dr. Paddon, in his 427-page memoir of the twenty-six years he spent living in Labrador, never once mentioned a wolverine, though he wrote about other wild animals at length. Likewise, the explorer Robinson, in his 155-page account of his expedition to Labrador, discussed in depth all kinds of animals he heard about or saw, but never made any mention of a wolverine. Dr. Grenfell, in his 434-page memoir of his life in Labrador, also didn't include any firsthand experience with a wolverine. He only alluded to them once indirectly, as part of a list of animals that had been trapped in the "early days" of the territory. Merrick too, in his memoir, which discussed hunting and trapping at length, never said anything about seeing wolverines, and only referred to them through two brief secondhand accounts.

But it's possible that wolverines were around, sometimes right under their noses, without their knowing it. Taking a second look at the descriptions from Traverspine with this in mind, they start to come into clearer focus—they seem to have all the hallmarks of the wolverine's mischievous behaviour. As might be expected from something that caused much excitement and alarm, the accounts agree on some points, but disagree on others. Adding to the confusion and difficulty of separating fact from fiction is that the local trappers themselves, including the Michelin family, never made any written records of their own. Living as they did in the wilderness, they had little formal education and little opportunity to write anything. Thus, we're left with the accounts made by those who stayed in the area or visited: the missionary doctors Grenfell, Paddon, and Forsyth, the adventurer Merrick and explorer Robinson, and lastly the wildlife biologist Wright—none of which agree exactly on the details of what stalked the woods around Traverspine.

Of the various testimonies, Paddon's and Forsyth's seem to hold particular weight, given that they each spent several decades residing in Labrador, in the process becoming respected members and integral parts of the isolated communities they served. As medical doctors, too, they were trained to observe things closely and to minutely record what they saw. Dr. Forsyth's account of the mysterious creature included these details about its tracks found in various places: "The trail usually runs out on glare ice or in running water. But such trails have been followed as much as fifteen miles over rough country. Whatever made them climbed easily over stumps and other obstructions where an ordinary man would have gone around. And whatever it was walked on two feet." Wolverines are highly agile and travel vast distances; there's no question that they're capable of climbing over stumps, rocks, and other obstructions that would force a person to go around. Wolverine trails can also lead over ice or across running water, and they are notoriously difficult animals to track. The only aspect of Dr. Forsyth's description that doesn't match a wolverine is the supposedly bipedal (two-footed) nature of the tracks. Although wolverines can stand on their hind legs and even walk like that for short distances, normally they walk on all fours.

But tracks can be misleading, particularly in deep or fresh snow. The tracks of a four-legged animal can appear as if they were made by a two-legged animal, given that in snow a wolverine, like most animals, will naturally place its hind paws in the same place as its forepaws, in effect doubling up its tracks. In deep snow or snow that has been disturbed by the wind, which erodes and obscures the edges of the track, wolverine prints can appear as giant barefooted human tracks—exactly as Dr. Forsyth had described them. He had differed from the others on this point in stating that the "stories are based on many reports of giant barefoot tracks in the snow." Moreover, given the wolverine's extreme rarity, even experts can misidentify their tracks.

Analyzing Forsyth's colleague and fellow physician Dr. Paddon's description of the incident reveals further clues that seem to point toward a wolverine. Paddon recalled that:

> the creature avoided the place by day but haunted it by night . . . Watch was kept from places of concealment at night, but without result . . . The creature evidently had a mate, as double tracks were seen, and also sounds of domestic strife were heard, with loud lamentations from the weaker member. No capture or killing was ever effected, and the affair remained a mystery.

The uncanny ability to avoid detection is another hallmark of wolverines. But the apparent mating behaviour is an even more significant piece of evidence. It seems to point toward actual animals rather than anything supernatural. From the little that's known about wolverine mating habits, the behaviour described by Paddon seems an exact match. Normally, wolverines are solitary and will even fight each other if they happen to cross paths; they generally tolerate each other's presence only for a few days during mating. Male wolverines are much larger than females, and on the rare occasions scientists have been able to observe wolverines mating in the wild, their behaviour has been described as involving aggressive snarling and biting and loud "screaming" by the females. Equipped with this knowledge, Paddon's statement that "sounds of domestic strife were heard, with loud lamentations from the weaker member" takes on new significance—it seems to point squarely at wolverines.

Naturally the notion that the Traverspine creature might have been a wolverine never occurred to Paddon or Forsyth, since neither of them had any experience with wolverines. But even Merrick's account, which seems a little more literary and perhaps embellished, contains clues that are highly suggestive of a wolverine. Again we hear of the uncanny ability to avoid baited traps, dropping to all fours, and lastly, ripping up logs looking for grubs, which is something wolverines do, as they'll eat just about anything, including insect larvae found in logs. Merrick's description of the creature has other details, too, that seem to further match a wolverine:

> ... she saw come out of the woods a huge hairy thing with low-hanging arms ... Across the top of its head was a white mane. She said it grinned at her, and she could see its white teeth ... They set bear traps for it, but it would never go near them. It ripped the bark off trees and rooted up huge rotten logs as though it were looking for grubs ... She says too that it had a ruff of white across the top of its head.

A wolverine's snarl would show off its very large teeth, which could explain the "grinning." Wolverines also have long limbs, which, depending on their posture, can make them look almost chimpanzee-like. Allowing for some degree of exaggeration or confusion in the darkened woods as well as the passage of time (over twenty years from the time it happened to when Merrick wrote it down), the description overall actually seems very suggestive of a wolverine. Mrs. Michelin (the woman who'd fired at the creature) too had insisted that, whatever it was, it wasn't a bear, which was an animal she knew well, having, in her own words, killed many. But she'd probably never seen a wolverine, and especially in the dark and thick brush, likely wouldn't have recognized one.

Indeed, even today experts can mistake wolverines for something else. The wildlife biologist Michel Huot notes that they can easily be mistaken for fishers (another large member of the weasel family), or small bears. Huot, in a recent interview about wolverines, explained, "The first time I saw a wolverine in a zoo, I was sure it was a fisher—and I had studied the animal extensively." If even an expert like Huot could misidentify one up close in broad daylight, it's easy to see how someone who'd only caught a glimpse of one half-screened in thick brush wouldn't recognize it, especially if they'd never seen one before.

But the eyewitnesses at Traverspine did get one detail exactly right—the white markings across the top of the head. The white patterning across the forehead is one of the wolverine's most distinctive characteristics. This detail had been mentioned by both Merrick and Professor Wright, the wildlife biologist. When I myself once saw a wolverine hiding in thick spruce branches, it was also the creature's white stripe that had most vividly impressed itself in my own memory.

Finally, analyzing Professor's Wright account of the Traverspine creature, which was based on the interviews he made with locals around Lake Melville, including Mrs. Michelin, brings additional clues to light that point to a wolverine. She again told Wright about the distinctive white blaze or stripe across the forehead, recalling, "It seemed to have a sort of white ruff across the top of its head, I could not make out the rest."

Wright also recorded the same detail about rooting up rotten logs as if "searching for grubs," and sometimes standing erect on their hind legs, but also running "on all fours"—all things wolverines do. Notably, too, Wright, like Dr. Paddon, reported that there were a male and female, stating: "These two strange animals, which the inhabitants called 'the man' and 'the woman' because one was larger than the other, stayed about the settlement despite attempts to trap them and drive them away." Male wolverines are much larger than females by a factor of about thirty percent, so this again seems to be compelling evidence pointing toward wolverines. It also doesn't seem like a detail a prankster would think to invent if they were merely making up spooky stories.

Another significant piece of evidence is the comment that the creatures had "cleaned up" seal bones "too big for the dogs." With their powerful jaws wolverines have been documented biting through even frozen moose bones, and could therefore easily make quick work of any seal bones. Wolverines have also been documented facing off against wolves and even driving them off their kills, which matches the detail recorded by Wright (and the others) that the mysterious creature "drove the dogs to a frenzy." Again, Mrs. Michelin and the others had insisted that whatever it was, it wasn't a bear, which if my wolverine theory is correct, she may have been right about after all. As Mrs. Michelin had insisted, "It was no bear . . . I saw enough of this thing to be sure of that."

Digging a little deeper into Labrador's past, further evidence emerges to indicate that wolverines inspired all kinds of strange beliefs and legends. Earlier in the 1890s, the surveyor Low reported that, at least in northern Labrador, over seven hundred kilometres north of Traverspine, the local Inuit and Naskapi trappers still occasionally encountered wolverines, which were so crafty, elusive, and tough that they were believed to have supernatural attributes. Low wrote of the wolverine in 1894:

> This animal is the personification of the devil among the Indians, owning to its cunning and destructive habits. Every Indian has wonderful stories to relate about the ferocity and intelligence of the wolverine. No cache of provisions or outfit is safe from the attacks of these animals, unless built up from the ground on high posts, in such a manner that the floors project and prevent the animals from reaching the sides or top. When a wolverine breaks into a cache, it not only eats the provisions, but breaks up and destroys other articles not fit for food.

Low gave several examples of wolverines in the area around Lake Melville, and their uncanny ability to not only avoid traps but to steal food from them without being caught in their iron jaws.

Low's comment that the wolverine was considered "the personification of the devil" is also highly interesting, given that it was just that word that the settlers at Traverspine had used to refer to the creature that had appeared around their houses. Is this merely a coincidence? Perhaps, but as noted earlier it's telling that in many places across North America wolverines were traditionally known by names with "devil" or "demon" in them. The anthropologist Frank Speck, who studied Naskapi culture in Labrador in the 1930s, also reported that Naskapi traditional beliefs regarded the wolverine as a malevolent, super-natural being. Indeed, not only in Labrador, but all across its native range, from North America to northern Scandinavia to the wilds of Russia, different cultures had myths and legends about wolverines that often associated it with evil spirits, the supernatural, and shape-shifting abilities.

If this was the case among cultures and fur trappers with firsthand knowledge of wolverines, one can only imagine what frightened children or settlers with little experience of wolver-ines would have made of the sudden appearance of one in their neck of the woods. Some further idea of the legends and myths that wolverines inspired can be found in early natural-ist accounts from elsewhere in North America. The explorer Jonathan Carver, for example, wrote in 1778 that the carcajou (the French name for the wolverine) was a fearsome creature that lurked in trees, lunging from them onto moose, caribou, and other prey, which it killed by strangling them with its tail. Compared to this, the Traverspine accounts seem almost tame in their descriptions.

These bizarre beliefs were a mixture of fact and fantasy, passed on and further garbled up around shared campfires—something that undoubtedly must have happened in Labrador, too, with the tales about the strange creature or creatures that had appeared at Traverspine told and retold until they became distorted or embellished. Wolverines do in fact climb trees, and they can kill even full-grown elk by jumping onto their backs and attacking the neck with their strong jaws—but certainly not with their tails. Another early traveller, the French Jesuit

Pierre-François-Xavier de Charlevoix, had even more bizarre ideas about wolverines. He described them as "a sort of wild Cat," and said that they were "the most terrible of all" predators. They even had, according to Charlevoix, strange powers that allowed them to control other animals, in particular foxes, which they employed to aid in their own hunting. Like Carver, Charlevoix also believed the wolverine had an exceptionally long tail; "it can twist it several times round its body" is how he put it. Charlevoix stated that its long tail was used to kill elk by strangling them and ripping open their jugulars.

Another early source written in 1917 by the naturalist Harold Elmer Anthony provides more evidence of how wolverines were peculiarly apt to give rise to wild legends, including ones involving supernatural attributes. Anthony noted of the wolverine that it has been:

> the subject of more legends and quaint stories than almost any other animal. According to the Indians, it is inhabited by an evil spirit. The French Canadians also gave it strange characteristics, under the name of Carcajou. In fact, the myths clustering about this animal date back as early as the sixteenth century in Europe.

Among these beliefs, wrote Anthony, were that wolverines were "ravenous monsters" that possessed "matchless strength" and "supernatural cunning," and were "a terror to all other beasts, the bloodthirsty master of the forest." Anthony also noted that among trappers, wolverines were thought to be as "cunning as the very Devil." Similarly, in eastern North America among the

Algonquian peoples, it was believed that wolverines could rise from the dead despite being slain many times—a legend that probably reflected how difficult it could be to kill a wolverine. Given all this, it seems little wonder then that in a place like Labrador, a century ago when access to natural history books or other sources were limited, and superstitions strong, the appearance of wolverines apparently set off wild rumours of phantom beasts haunting the forests.

Examining all the evidence carefully, it seemed clear to me that a wolverine was at least partly behind the Traverspine legend. It matched the descriptions closely, and more so than any other candidate, and since it was mysterious and extremely rare, it was very likely to have inspired embellishments about it among the local settlers in Labrador—just as it did elsewhere. Sitting around our campfire, I told Zach my wolverine theory and explained my reasoning.

"When you put it like that," Zach nodded, "it makes perfect sense. And the same thought had actually crossed my mind when I'd read about the white stripe on the head. But I figured it couldn't be because of the size difference. A wolverine standing on its hind legs wouldn't be much more than four feet. But didn't they say it was seven feet tall?"

"A few did," I said, "but I think that has to be taken with a grain of salt, given that it was based on the eyewitness account provided by the little girl who saw it on the edge of the clearing. In the eyes of a frightened child, any animal would likely seem much larger than it actually was. Also, when Mrs. Michelin saw it, she said it was hidden in the bushes, implying that it could have been on higher ground or standing on a log or rock or what have you. And at a distance and in the confusion of the moment, accurately estimating size wouldn't be easy."

"That's true," agreed Zach.

"Plus, in the more than twenty years between when the sighting happened and when Merrick wrote it down, the details in the story were likely changed or embellished with each retelling."

"Naturally," said Zach. "Now what?"

"I was thinking we should explore more of the mountain and look for caves, to see if we can find a wolverine in any," I said.

"Crawl face-first into a cave to see if a wolverine is in it? Sounds like a wonderful idea," nodded Zach.

"Exactly. Now we best get going, there's a lot of ground to cover," I said.

Feeling confident that we'd unravelled at least part of the mystery, Zach and I took a camera, our water bottles, a few snacks, and the bear spray, and set off from our camp to see what we could find.

21

OVER THE MOUNTAINS

Language fails to paint the awful desolation
of the table-land of the Labrador Peninsula.
—Henry Youle Hind, *The Northwest Territory*, 1864

WE HEADED ACROSS the mountain plateau, climbing and scrambling over rock outcrops and cliffs, as well as plunging through sheltered gullies where alpine dwarf spruce grew in dense thickets. Our plan was to work our way to the western slopes of the mountain, where we suspected we'd find more caves. As we went, we paused to snack on wild berries and admire the sweeping views of rugged wilderness unfolding in all directions to the horizon. Fortunately, we found another small cleft in the rocks filled with cold water, where we were able to replenish our bottles.

It was a cold day; we both had on our warm gloves and wool toques. The skies were grey and overcast, the wind fierce. When we reached the far side of the mountain, we found immense boulders of grey rock that had split off the mountain face and tumbled far below. Zach and I edged our way cautiously along stupendous drop-offs and precipitous cliffs, searching for any cave openings.

Wolverines will make their homes in a variety of habitats: ranging from snowdrifts to holes they dig themselves under uprooted trees, and even old bear or wolf dens. On only two occasions had I encountered wolverines in the wild, and I considered myself lucky to have done so at all. Both times were deep in the wilderness of the Northwest Territories, hundreds of miles from the nearest town or road.

The first occasion was while on an expedition with a sole companion, my good friend Chuck. We'd been canoeing for weeks up an isolated, winding river north of Great Bear Lake when coming around a river bend, we spotted something we at first could hardly believe. Concealed within the branches of a towering spruce was the vague outline of some dark shadow, from which gleamed a pair of intense eyes, staring right at us. I focused my gaze and saw that, whatever the thing was, running across its black body was a white marking. We paddled toward the bank for a closer look. My first thought was that it might be a young bear that had climbed the tree. But as we approached, the creature manoeuvred in the branches, and I realized to my surprise that we'd encountered one of the rarest and most elusive animals: a wolverine. That wasn't all: as we watched this small bear-like animal, I noticed there were *two* wolverines concealed in the shadows of the spruce. It looked like they were young ones, although they seemed quite large and must have been nearly full-grown. The two wolverines stared at my companion and me for a few minutes, before climbing swiftly down the tree and disappearing into the forest. Fortunately, I had my camera with me, and aimed and snapped a few photos of the tree, which allowed me to zoom in later and verify that they'd indeed been wolverines—otherwise I'm not sure I'd have believed it.

The only other occasion I'd seen a wolverine in the wild was while canoeing the remote Anderson River en route to the icy Beaufort Sea, when from the stern of my canoe I glimpsed one moving along a bank in the distance. It had quickly disappeared into the spruce woods, and after we'd landed the canoe, we could find no trace of it. In all my other months of wandering across the wilderness, I'd never seen another, though once when mapping rivers in the subarctic, I found a possible den site near the coast of Hudson Bay.

"There's a cave over there," said Zach, snapping me out of my daydream. He pointed across a gully in the mountainside to a dark entrance on a cliff face.

"That looks promising," I said.

"Very promising ... for getting our faces ripped off by a wolverine," observed Zach.

We carefully scrambled our way along the cliffs, climbing over boulders and occasionally leaping across small gaps in the rock to reach the cave entrance. I edged forward toward the shadowy opening in the ancient rocks, then, half expecting a demon creature to jump out at me, peered into the gloom.

"It's empty," I said.

"Darn, well there's plenty more caves ahead," replied Zach.

We continued working our way across the mountain, inspecting various caves, mostly of small size, as we crept along. It was exhausting work, scrambling up and down the rocks, and battling the winds as we did so. Huffing and puffing, we came to a rock ledge and rested for a few moments, taking in the magnificent view. Mountain summits rose above the dark green forests below, stretching endlessly away before us. Far across a forested valley, on a remote cliff face partway up the slope of a high mountain, we could see a much larger cave. It looked like a perfect place for something to live undetected by the modern world.

"You know," said Zach, sipping from his water bottle, "something has been bothering me. What about those cloven hoof tracks? There's no way a wolverine track could be mistaken for a cloven hoof. Several of those accounts had been very insistent about the tracks."

"The same thought has been nagging me at the back of my mind," I admitted.

Of the six contemporary or near contemporary accounts of the Traverspine creature(s), half had said the tracks were in the shape of cloven hoofs. "Cloven," meaning split down the middle, are the kind of tracks made by goats and ox. Tradition had long associated cloven hoofs with demons or the Devil (a fact reflected in the common depiction of the Devil with the lower half of a goat). But there were no farm animals in Traverspine, and if by chance some had wound up there, they couldn't have lasted long without being tracked, especially since all the trapping families kept keen-nosed huskies as sled dogs.

The explorer Robinson had described the tracks in the most detail. Recalling that "the trail of some mysterious animal" had been found one day near Traverspine, he stated:

> The footmarks were long, and had two toes. The creatures must have been very heavy, because the marks were sunk into the ground deeply in places where the footmarks of a man would hardly leave any trace … the animal seemed to be a biped, and the length of the step was about four feet. It was

near the River Traverspine . . . where first the footmarks were seen, and right along the side of the river, which was low at the time, the prints could be traced for miles. There were very few men about, but every one who was there went and had a look at these footprints, and they got very much disturbed in mind about this strange trail.

Dr. Grenfell, who'd been anchored in his ship on Lake Melville, had also recalled the strange incident in his memoir, published about ten years after Robinson's account. Grenfell stated that a fur trader from Revillon Frères, a French fur company with a post on Lake Melville, had seen the tracks with a "Scotch settler" outside the latter's cabin (which may have actually been the Michelins). In Grenfell's words, "They had tracked it, measured the footmarks in the mud, and even fenced some of them round. The stride was about eight feet, the marks as of the cloven hoofs of an ox." In Grenfell's recollection the creature's stride had doubled from four feet to eight feet, but the shape of the tracks was consistent. Leaving that aside, the fact remains that both Robinson and Grenfell had described the tracks as cloven hoofed.

Merrick, too, had described them as such and had even said he'd seen paper cut-outs of their shape. Merrick's account was made in 1930, fully twenty years after Robinson's. He'd become close friends with the Michelins and other families clustered around Lake Melville, and had spent that winter trapping together with one of them. In his account of what he called the "Traverspine Gorilla," Merrick noted that the tracks were "everywhere" in the mud, and later in the snow:

They measured the tracks and cut out paper patterns of them which they still keep. It is a strange-looking foot, about twelve inches long, narrow at the heel and forking at the front into two broad, round-ended toes. Sometimes its print was so deep it looked to weigh five hundred pounds. At other times the beast's mark looked no deeper than a man's track.

Merrick further stated that over a dozen people had told him they had personally seen the strange tracks.

On the other hand, Dr. Paddon, Dr. Forsyth, and Professor Wright hadn't said anything about cloven hoofs in their accounts. Forsyth had said the tracks were "giant barefoot" tracks although he didn't mention anything about their being found at Traverspine, and it seems he may have been referring to ones found elsewhere. His colleague, Paddon, while agreeing with the others that "tracks were found of which patterns were preserved" at Traverspine, also didn't specify what shape the tracks took. However, he seemed to imply that the tracks were more ape-like than hoofed. Wright likewise said the tracks were "twelve inches long indicating great weight," but didn't mention anything about hoofs. Despite believing that it had been a grizzly bear, Wright conceded that the tracks were the most puzzling aspect of the affair.

Tallying up these accounts, half said they were cloven hoofed, and half either said or implied that they looked vaguely primate or bear-like. What are we to make of these contradictions? Of course, they might suggest the fallibility of human memory and the tendency to confuse or distort events over time. But I think the evidence suggests that there's more to it than just that. If there'd been only one account on either side, we might assume that the author had simply been mistaken or else was making things up. But given the existence of three collaborating accounts on either side made independently of each other, it seems clear that they must have had some basis in actual events—for instance, encounters with some other unfamiliar animal, not a wolverine, but something else entirely.

I thought about everything I knew of monster legends and folklore. Legends of things that go bump in the night were often derived from composites of one or more real animals—frequently animals that were rare or unfamiliar or had strayed outside their typical range. Known as a "chimera" from the ancient Greek term, these folk creatures were rooted in confused and garbled up components from actual creatures. Could the Traverspine beast have been a composite of different animals? Primarily something that had been inspired by a wolverine, but that had gradually, over time, been partly mixed up with some other creature?

For example, a well-known monster of Australian tradition, the fearsome bunyip, was believed to lurk in freshwater rivers and swamps. Said to have a hideous, gigantic dog-like appearance, with whiskers, flippers, bulging eyes, and a brightly coloured chest, it was reputed to lay greenish-blue eggs of great size, leave marks with sharp claws, and emit a haunting, booming call at night. Accounts of such a bizarre creature were made throughout the 1800s and early 1900s in Australia—and given that continent's unusual wildlife, such as the platypus, many simply accepted that the bunyip was a real animal. But later investigations revealed no such creature; instead, naturalists and wildlife experts posit that the legend of the bunyip developed based on occasional sightings of rare animals unfamiliar to most Australians.

The giant size, bulging eyes, whiskers, and flippers, as well as the marine habitat, are all characteristic of seals—including leopard seals, a predatory species that can measure up to twelve feet long and weigh over thirteen hundred pounds, with impressive canines that allow it to kill and eat other seals. These giant marine creatures normally live in Antarctic waters and breed on isolated islands, but they have occasionally strayed into Australia. Leopard seals have been found in Australia's Murray and Darling rivers, two locations where the bunyip was historically sighted. The bunyip's other characteristics—greenish-blue eggs of great size, sharp claws, brightly coloured chest, and booming night call—were traits borrowed from encounters with two rare birds: the southern cassowary, a large flightless bird related to ostriches with spear-like feet that lays giant greenish-blue eggs, and the Australasian bittern, a seldom seen nocturnal bird that lives in marshes and makes a booming call. Occasional encounters with these rare or unfamiliar creatures provided all the component parts for the legend of the bunyip.

It's easy to imagine how something like this might happen over time. One day a group of hunters spot something they've never seen before swimming in the river, glimpsing it from a distance. That sighting gets preserved in oral tradition, a tale told and retold around countless campfires, until gradually other details are added. Maybe on another occasion someone finds the crushed remains of a giant greenish-blue egg, or strange tracks that look like dinosaur claws, and these unaccountable things get bundled up as belonging to the creature spotted years earlier. Later still, maybe someone else hears a haunting, booming call echoing out of the marshes, and never having seen a bittern during the daylight (since they're exceedingly rare nocturnal creatures), attributes the frightening call to the same mystery creature spotted once long ago in the river. Eventually, all the different ingredients get so thoroughly intertwined that they become inseparable, and just like that, a monster myth is born. If it could happen in Australia, it wasn't hard to imagine something similar happening in Labrador's wilderness.

Indeed, this same phenomenon has played out elsewhere. Another example of how a chimera legend can form may be Scotland's Loch Ness monster. Although it's reputed to be a prehistoric-looking sea creature with a long neck and slimy back, scientists think, after extensively analyzing Loch Ness and all the species that live in it, that the legend was in fact based on sightings of large eels, which are numerous in the lake, along with swimming roe deer. When seen from a distance or in dim light, the silhouette of a swimming deer actually looks remarkably like the eyewitness descriptions of the supposed Loch Ness monster, with its long neck above the waterline. Occasional sightings of eels swimming near the surface would supply the remaining details. Mixed together over the years, the result is a folklore creature that doesn't exist in the flesh, but instead, like the Australian bunyip, it's a legend combining parts of different real animals into a single creature.

Another example that illustrates how this might happen can be found on the walls of prehistoric caves in Greece. Some of these cave paintings depict centaurs: mythical animals that were believed to have the lower half of a horse and the upper half of a human. Thousands of years ago, when these paintings were made, there weren't any horses in Europe. Wild horses were native to the steppes of central Asia, near modern Mongolia and Kazakhstan. Imagine, then, a group of ancient Greek wanderers venturing far from their homeland and glimpsing, perhaps from some vantage point on high ground, an unknown tribe riding an unknown animal. From a distance, without the benefit of binoculars, a shirtless rider on a horse without a saddle could easily be mistaken for a single animal. Returning home to their little villages back in Greece, the travellers would have told of the strange creatures they'd seen with the upper half of a human, and the lower half of a horse. The story would get recorded in cave paintings and elsewhere, and like that, the myth of the centaur is born.

A fourth chimera legend is probably the werewolf. As partly explained earlier, belief in the werewolf flourished in medieval and Renaissance Europe, a time when wolf attacks were a very real threat that peasants and shepherds faced. Every year hundreds of shepherds and peasants were killed by wolves. But wolves weren't the only danger people faced. There were also, just as there are today, rare but horrifying cases of human murderers and serial killers, who might mutilate their victims or engage in all kinds of disturbing behaviour. One of the most infamous was Peter Stumpf, a sixteenth-century German farmer who became known as "The Werewolf of Bedburg." Stumpf confessed to murdering and eating sixteen people. He was branded a werewolf and executed, his limbs smashed with a blunt side of an axe in order to hinder his ability to rise from the grave. News of such macabre cases spread like wildfire, and in a land of medieval superstition, vast forests, and limited crime investigative techniques, actual human murders could easily get mixed up and entwined with all-too-frequent wolf attacks in the wild hinterlands, fusing together to give rise to werewolf legends—half man, half wolf creatures that supposedly prowled the countryside.

These examples sharpened my thinking about Traverspine. It seemed clear that the accounts weren't purely made up or hoaxes; they seemed to have had some foundation in wolverines that had become mixed up with some other mystery animal, eventually conflating them into a single thing. That this might be the case was in part evidenced by the disagreement over the dates when the sightings had occurred. Robinson described a single incident that occurred sometime before 1909, and Grenfell implied something similar. But Merrick had stated that the creature had haunted Traverspine over a longer period: for "two winters," as he put it. Even more divergent were Dr. Paddon, Dr. Forsyth, and Professor Wright, each of whom implied that the sightings and findings of tracks took place over a much longer period of time spanning decades, and over a much wider geographic distribution than just Traverspine. Professor Wright had said that the last sighting had occurred in 1940, more than thirty years after Robinson's report.

If much of the accounts, especially the ones featuring the human/bear-like tracks, were based on wolverines, where did the rest of the details come from? Were the cloven hoofs just pure imagination or hallucinations? I think the evidence suggests that they were in fact based on something quite real that had wandered into the vast forests around Traverspine, something that the local settlers had never seen before, and probably never did again. What might that have been?

22

MONSTERS OF THE WILD

Dark and desolate lies the sand
Along the wastes of a barren land
—Thomas S. Collier, "Off Labrador," 1832

IT SOMETIMES SEEMS that the simplest explanations, the ones right under our noses, are the hardest to see. The answer to the other half of the Traverspine mystery was contained within the pages of all the fur trade records, diaries, and memoirs I'd been studying for weeks. These sources were rich in detail about the wildlife of Labrador, discussing many different animals at length. But, like the wolverine, another animal was conspicuous by its total absence from any historical record of the region.

Reading the cloven hoof descriptions in the clear light of day, it's unmistakable what they're describing, albeit unknowingly: *moose tracks*. Simply put, the accounts are a dead ringer for the giant cloven hoof tracks made by a moose. But how could it be that none of the local Labradorians, born and bred trappers as they were, failed to recognize them as such? The answer is simple: they'd never seen moose before, because historically moose didn't range into Labrador. There are no records of moose at all in

Labrador prior to the 1950s, when they were intentionally transported and released there. Under normal circumstances, the nearest moose were far south of Labrador.

The trappers and hunters of Labrador a century ago were experts at their craft, but the only member of the deer family that historically lived in Labrador was caribou. Elk, moose, white-tailed deer, and mule deer all lived far to the south and west. The conditions in Labrador, with its barren mountains, windswept tundra, and harsh environment, weren't suitable for these other species, which require different habitat types. Over the course of their lives, Labrador trappers killed hundreds of caribou, often tracking them across frozen lakes or into the mountains. But moose were never seen or reported anywhere in the territory.

Today, however, more than a hundred years later, moose have become relatively common in Labrador. That's because in 1953, twelve moose were deliberately released in southern Labrador as part of a government program to replace the caribou that, by that time, had been hunted almost to extinction. Given changes in snow cover, the introduced moose were able to find enough of their natural food sources in the more sheltered river valleys. They were able to adapt and thrive, and have gradually multiplied to the point where they're now common.

Among my copious photocopies was a study from the 1960s on the introduction of moose into Labrador. It corroborated what I'd already concluded based on my other reading: that earlier residents of Labrador had no previous familiarity with moose. As the authors of the study noted, "The first moose to be recorded in the Goose Bay area was observed by Mr. John

Blake ... on the Churchill River, in late fall, 1961." That wasn't far from Traverspine; the Blakes were a well-known Labrador trapper family with roots in the area going back centuries. John Blake, who'd seen the moose, told the researchers it was the first he'd ever seen and at the time he didn't know what it was: "He stated that this animal (a bull) was the first moose that he had seen and that when he saw it he did not know what it was."

If even in the 1960s, old-time Labrador trappers didn't recognize moose, it makes it easier to appreciate how, for the trappers and hunters of Merrick's time, they were virtually unknown. Indeed, Grenfell, Merrick, Paddon, and Robinson never mentioned moose at all, not even once in the thousands of pages of their memoirs describing life in Labrador—nor did any other fur trade report, oral tale, or anything else I could find on historical Labrador. Yet they all discussed caribou multiple times. This was surely hugely significant—not once in a lifetime did any of these people see a moose in the Labrador woods.

But sometime in the early 1900s, by chance, it seems, a moose or two must have wandered north from the Laurentian Mountains of Quebec and appeared around Traverspine, causing confusion and bewilderment with its massive cloven hoof tracks that were vastly larger and sunk deeper into the earth than any caribou track ever could be. Accustomed as they were to a lifetime spent tracking caribou, to suddenly see out of nowhere the vastly larger, gigantic tracks of a moose—which are indeed cloven hoofed and of the huge dimensions mentioned in the accounts, as moose are more than three times heavier than a caribou—would certainly be startling. I could appreciate this from my own experience.

In the woods that surrounded my childhood home white-tailed deer were abundant, and so from an early age I became accustomed to encountering their tracks. But there weren't any moose in my family's woods, and it wasn't until later that I came across the tracks of one for the first time. Compared to the deer tracks I was familiar with they seemed shockingly large—monstrously larger than any deer track, like a kind of Godzilla of white-tailed deer, and sunk far deeper into the ground. And the stride of a moose really is truly gigantic—about two metres. Of course, I had the advantage of animal tracking guide books and other resources at my fingertips. But even today, when I've since encountered hundreds of moose tracks in the woods, they still astonish me with their sheer size. These experiences let me appreciate the feelings of those Labrador trappers long ago.

Nowadays, most of us take it for granted that when we meet with something unknown, we can simply look up the answer online, or at the very least, consult a book or phone someone. None of this, however, was available a century ago in the isolated frontier homesteads of Labrador. Knowledge, in essence, was restricted to one's lived experience. This made people masters of their environment, but it also meant perplexity and confusion when something that didn't belong there suddenly appeared—as seemed to have happened at Traverspine. The Michelins and other Labrador trapping families had lived in Labrador for generations and had no experience of the fauna species found elsewhere in Canada. Ironically, it was their own expertise in the Labrador woods that defeated their efforts to identify the tracks—since moose didn't normally occur in Labrador. The historical accounts I'd studied mentioned that most settlers had only a single book in their simple homes—the family Bible. When confronted with the giant, unknown tracks, they'd turned to the explanation their religious traditions offered: the cloven hoofs were the tracks of the "Devil" or "one of his agents."

Rereading Robinson's account (the first one made of the Traverspine beast) with this knowledge, it actually seems a rather straightforward and ordinary description of a moose. Of course, Robinson was from Britain, so he had no more familiarity or experience with moose tracks than the local Labradorians. Robinson had related:

> Joe Mesher [meaning Michelin] is the name of the huntsman who first found the trail of some mysterious animal. The footmarks were long, and had two toes. The creatures must have been very heavy, because the marks were sunk into the ground deeply in places where the footmarks of a man would hardly leave any trace.

This is exactly what moose tracks look like; they're long, sink deeply into the earth, and appear to have two toes. Robinson continued:

> ... the animal seemed to be a biped, and the length of the step was about four feet. It was near the River Traverspine ... where first the footmarks were seen, and right along the side of the river, which was low at the time, the prints could be traced for miles. There were very few men about, but every one who was there went and had a look at these footprints, and they got very much disturbed in mind about this strange trail.

Moose normally walk along muddy shorelines, as alders and aquatic vegetation comprise much of their diet (more than once when camping on a riverbank I've had one loudly wake me up). They of course aren't bipedal (two-legged), but to someone unfamiliar with their tracks, they can appear as if made by a two-legged animal.

Robinson went on: "The next to be heard of this strange visitor was one night when the huntsman's wife was alone. She described the noise as a 'rumbling sort of whistling noise like breathing,' and now and again branches of trees were snapped." Moose, like horses and elk, do produce a snorting, whining, and rumbling call with their huge snouts, which I knew from experience could be quite an eerie thing to hear when you're alone in the woods in the dark. Moose also snap tree branches exactly as described in the account. You can always tell where a moose has been by the broken-off branches it leaves in its wake.

Robinson continued: "Outside the house she found all the dogs shivering with fear. It was too dark to see anything distinctly, so she let fly a chance shot amongst the trees. Immediately there was a crashing of branches, and the sound of some huge monster tearing hotly away." The dogs may have been frightened by the scent of a large, unfamiliar animal (a moose can weigh up to sixteen hundred pounds), but this may also have simply been an exaggeration. In any case, the description of crashing branches sounds exactly like a startled moose running off through thick brush. No matter how many times I myself have startled a moose in the woods, the racket they make as they run off through the undergrowth, knocking trees aside in the process, always gets my heart pumping. Robinson further explained:

On the afternoon of the following day her husband returned, and with him was a mate from down the river, to whom he had been to fetch a barrel of flour, as his provisions were running short. Together they went into the woods, accompanied by the wife. They found that some enormous creatures had been there, and traced the footprints quite down to the river. All the way down the branches of the trees were snapped and broken off. The footprints went straight into the river, and, of course, all trace was there lost.

Again, this is precisely like a moose, which naturally tends to go toward water (they regularly swim in order to seek out the underwater plants they like to feed on). The snapped and broken-off branches they found are another unmistakable moose sign. Moreover, when Zach and I camped at the ruins of Traverspine, those were exactly the sounds I heard in the early morning from inside my tent—sounds that turned out to be three moose, and they too had swum across the river. Robinson added:

There had evidently been two creatures this time, because the footmarks showed that, besides the large imprints, which were very deep wherever the soil was loose, there were small but similar marks alongside, but with a stretch of only about three feet between each step. It looked as if a mother and her young one had been there.

This sounds an awful lot like the tracks of a cow moose and her calf—just what Zach and I encountered at Traverspine more than a hundred years later. Although today, thanks to the government introduction of moose in the 1950s, they're not rare at all, but commonplace. The introduced moose multiped rapidly across Labrador and Newfoundland, replacing the caribou that had historically roamed the mountains and woods. In other words, stripped of its sensationalism, Robinson's account, the first one made of the Traverspine beast, actually reads like a rather ordinary description of a moose. Finally Robinson stated:

> The above is the sum and substance of what I was told, and more than a dozen men declare that when out hunting they have seen similar footprints . . . they did not like to say what really was in their minds, and that was that Monsieur le Diable had been taking his strolls around that quarter of the globe.

Robinson concluded that the creature was some sort of prehistoric relic that had survived deep in the wilderness of Labrador, and that before long, a new species would be discovered. But he had no more firsthand experience with moose than the Labrador trappers. Those tough, frontier trappers were brave and even fearless when it came to the familiar dangers they faced routinely: polar bears, black bears, and wolves, even the odd grizzly. But it's the unknown things we generally fear, the things we can't see that get the better of our imagination and cause it to run wild. A century ago in the wilds of Labrador, the moose and wolverine filled that role.

It seemed clear now, breathing in the pure mountain air, that the Traverspine beast was actually based on fleeting encounters with two rare and unfamiliar animals, which over time had become blended together through stories passed around shared campfires, until they gradually morphed into one thing in the tales. This is how most traditional folklore all over the world operates—oral tales told and retold, which in the beginning had some basis or grain of truth behind them, but over time become increasingly embellished. Like a giant game of telephone—the children's game where a message or phrase is whispered into another person's ear and passed down the line until the person at the end announces what they hear—it invariably ends up quite different from the original message. In this sense folklore is kind of like a mixed stew, in which different storytellers contribute different ingredients that all get tossed into the same pot, then stirred around and mixed up together. In Traverspine, nearly four decades spanned the earliest account, Robinson's in 1909 to the last one by a contemporary, Dr. Forsyth's in 1947—more than enough time for the story to get confused and intertwined.

It was clear, too, that the stories grew less realistic with the passage of time, a testament to the telephone effect and the fallibility of human memory. That this had happened was evident from the discrepancies contained in the accounts, contradictions that had become plainer to me the more I carefully scrutinized them. Eventually, Dr. Paddon's son, who was born years after the original incidents had occurred, recalled as an old man in his mid-seventies the Traverspine beast in a book he published about his life growing up in Labrador. By that point the details had morphed almost beyond recognition from the original story. Paddon junior said that a "sasquatch" had once been seen at Traverspine—a name that came from British Columbia and had little connection to the original accounts.

In sum, folk monsters frequently take the form of chimeras—legendary creatures that are based on combining two ordinary things, as was the case with the Australian bunyip. The Traverspine beast was a local Labradorian version; a chimera based on two rare and unfamiliar animals, the wolverine and the moose, which together provided all the pieces of the fearsome creature. The white mane, the grinning teeth, the ability to bite clean through seal bones, to alternate from two legs to four, to avoid baited traps, and the strange mating behaviour were all the contributions of wolverines—incredibly rare and elusive creatures that few people ever saw. While the giant cloven hoof tracks sunk deep into the earth, the snapped-off branches seven feet off the ground, and the "rumbling, whistling" noise in the dark came from the moose side of the equation—animals that normally lived well south of Labrador, and which weren't historically known in the territory. Mixed up and combined over many an evening spent round a fire, as the years passed, the stories were written down by different chroniclers, becoming fused in the process into one terrifying, mysterious demon creature that stalked the woods.

But when calmly and dispassionately analyzed in the clear light of day, and with a modern knowledge of the natural history and wildlife biology of northeastern Canada, the fog around the legend evaporates, and it all seems very simple and clear. In Labrador a century ago, all the evidence suggests moose and wolverines were rare, unfamiliar animals outside the bounds of everyday experience.

I filled Zach in on my moose thoughts, and he nodded in agreement about it.

"Well, that clears that up," Zach said from his perch on a rock shelf, near the cliff edge.

"Yes, I think it does," I replied.

It seemed at last we'd unravelled and solved the mystery. We'd climbed the mountain hoping to find enlightenment, and we'd found it. With nothing further to do, and nothing more to trouble our sleep, it was time we started heading back.

23

ACROSS THE MARSHES

It is in vain to dream of a wildness distant from ourselves. There is none such. It is the bog in our brains and bowels, the primitive vigor of Nature in us, that inspires that dream. I shall never find in the wilds of Labrador a greater wildness than in some recess of Concord, i.e. than I import into it.
—Henry David Thoreau, *Journal*, 1852

Zach and I returned to our camp, took down our tents and packed everything up, ate some wild berries, and prepared for the long trek back to where we'd left our canoe and other gear. It was September in the mountains after all, and winter was coming. We couldn't delay our return any longer. The food we'd brought with us for our mountain trek had nearly run out; we were down to just a few freeze-dried meals and a couple of granola bars each. Plenty more food was waiting for us back at the barrel—that is, if a wolverine or bear hadn't already found it.

Neither of us relished the idea of retracing our route back through the haunted mountain valley where our sleep had been disturbed by strange noises—even if we did think the monster was little more than a wolverine and moose mixed up together. Nor did we wish to cut back through the torturous thickets, deadfall, and steep hills we'd faced on the way in if there was a way we could avoid it. Instead we figured we'd try our luck taking a different route back. Our plan was to head directly down the north face of the mountain, which was much more precipitous than the forested eastern slope we'd taken on the way up. But if we could find a way down the north face, we'd be able to avoid the mountain valley with the stream and its impenetrable thickets.

The skies were clouded over and the winds were stiff and cold. Standing on the cliff edge with our backpacks strapped on, the tents lashed to them, and our boots taped up so they wouldn't come undone, we scanned the horizon of vast forests spreading out before us, trying to determine the best route back. Unlike on our trek here, we now had the advantage of a bird's-eye view, which allowed us to roughly sketch out a hypothetical route across what looked like the least difficult terrain. Judging from what we could see from the summit, there appeared to be a long series of marshes or muskegs directly below the north face. Surprisingly enough we'd had quite a bit of luck crossing muskeg on the way here, and Zach and I were of the same opinion that we'd rather take our chances traversing more bogs on the way back than clawing our way through dense thickets. In the far distance, we could see the Kenemich River winding through the landscape like a giant anaconda. We had to make it there to reunite with our canoe.

"All we have to do," I said, pointing the route out, "is climb down the cliffs here without falling, find a way through the thickets at the bottom without getting lost, and then cut across all that muskeg without sinking. After that, if we stick northeast, we should reach those thickly forested hills on the horizon and rejoin our old route, and from there eventually find our way back to where we left the canoe."

"Piece of cake," said Zach.

Zach led the way down the mountain. I lingered a moment longer, taking a last look to commit as much of the route to memory as I could. We had to head north, then northeast, and finally north again. That done, I cast a final glance behind me at the mountain plateau with its giant boulders, its alpine spruces, its dark caves and crevices. I had a feeling that as long as I lived I'd never forget this place. When I turned back, Zach had already disappeared out of view down the steep slope.

I hiked off at a quick pace to catch up with him. Great slabs of ancient rock formed this side of the mountain, with hardly any vegetation growing on their barren, windswept surfaces. The rocks were steep, but we could descend them carefully by avoiding vertical drops and taking the easier routes.

Our progress down the rocks was quite rapid, and we soon reached the treeline, where balsam fir, black spruce, mountain ash, and birch were to be found. But even here, there were many sheer cliffs and very steep terrain. In fact, things were actually harder inside the treeline, since the trees screened our views, hiding abrupt cliff edges that we might suddenly plunge off as we blindly pushed through the bushes above them.

Several times Zach and I found ourselves emerging from the bushes immediately above cliff faces, where we had to climb laterally to find a less vertical route down. However, in a few places, we couldn't avoid them. Fortunately we were able to grasp onto the hardy little knarred spruces, only a few feet high, or else some slender birches, to support our weight and then lower ourselves down that way. Still, it was a little dicey, especially with our heavy packs. In a few places, we let ourselves drop several feet, catching ourselves against a tree before careening and tumbling wildly out of control down the mountainside. In other places, we dropped or rather dangled, right in front of caves which we hadn't seen from above as we came down the steep slope. This was a little bit nerve-racking, as if a bear happened to be in one it might amuse itself by swatting at us like a human piñata. Luckily, the caves were all empty as far as we could tell.

Eventually we reached the bottom of the mountain, where dense swamp forests awaited us. Here we wove between spruces and tamaracks until we came upon an area of giant ferns. The ferns were nearly as tall as our waists, and seemed somewhat out of place in the subarctic. I couldn't recall meeting with ferns this large in subarctic woods before. We pushed through the ferns until we reached the marshes, or bog, and then began our traverse of it. Crossing these muskegs the blackflies suddenly materialized again, attacking our faces, necks, behind our ears, and any other exposed skin they could get at with their itchy bites.

The sun was going down quickly, and it was clear we wouldn't make it all the way back to the canoe before dark. So we made the best of our situation, and camped in the middle of open muskeg, where the annoyance of the blood-sucking insects was at least compensated for by the magnificent view of the mountains behind us. They stood dark and mysterious-looking, wave upon wave of barren bluish peaks, the highest ones hidden in drifting cloud. The ground everywhere was marshy, but on the bright side it was soft.

We pitched our tents near a little pond on the driest patch of marsh we could find, which it turned out wasn't very dry at all. Rather than peg the tents down, which, given the plethora of soft mosses and lichens built up layer upon layer, wouldn't be very effective, we instead lashed them with guy lines to the tiny dwarf tamaracks. This gave the tents more support than the spongy ground could offer. White-throated sparrows chirped and sang amid the miniature dwarf tamaracks, while the rich fragrance of Labrador tea shrubs filled the air. There wasn't much firewood in the marsh, but we gathered whatever dead wood we could find for building a small fire to purify swamp water.

We sat on little lichen-covered hummocks, sipping tea by the sputtering fire and discussing the facts of the Traverspine mystery. It seemed we'd accounted for nearly everything.

"But what was that whispering noise in the night we heard?" Zach wondered.

"Just some trick of the wind echoing through the distant mountains," I said.

That reminded me of some of the Labrador oral histories I'd been studying. One of the more intriguing ones concerned a certain haunted place known as Savage Cove, on the far side of the Mealy Mountains, about a hundred and sixty kilometres from us. Many elderly Labradorians knew tales about this lonely spot, near where the Eagle River meets the sea. Back in the early twentieth century the area was supposedly haunted by what local families called the "Savage Cove Devil." The oral tales all described a terrifying half-crying, half-whispering scream that would issue from the dark woods surrounding this isolated cove. Others compared it to wolves' howling, only more evil sounding and screechy, alternating from low whispers to loud shrieks. Sometimes the eerie sound would echo for miles across the water, sending shivers down the spines of all who heard it.

The chilling sounds were heard for years at that spot, and while skeptics said it was only the wind and the rocks, some of the elders recalled how they'd heard the sound even on calm days, when the sea was smooth as glass and there was no wind. Some claimed it was the voices of ghosts that haunted the cove; others that a demon stalked the woods there. Dozens of respected, steady-minded trappers and others testified that they heard the strange, unearthly noises. Almost everyone avoided the cove, giving it a wide berth on their trips into the bay.

Finally, one day a trapper of more than ordinary courage resolved to make a thorough investigation of the haunted cove. He and a companion rowed ashore under darkness, and flashlights in hand, followed the eerie sound up a small hill. Here was a little brook flowing down; they could hear the screeching noise issuing from somewhere nearby. Eventually they found what was causing it: a big tree had partly uprooted near the brook. Its roots were reaching into the water, meaning the stream's current would shake the tree, making it creak and groan in the process. When it was windy the sounds were magnified, creating the unholy screams. The next morning at first light the two trappers returned with an axe and chopped down the tree, so that no one would be troubled by the ghostly sounds again.

More than likely, I thought to myself, the noises we'd heard on the night wind in the wooded valley were something similar. Plus, our own dehydration and exhaustion had probably contributed to whatever we thought we'd heard in the darkness.

Our fire burned low, the last glowing embers slowly dying away. The sun had sunk below the mountains while the black-flies had vanished as the temperature plunged. We crawled into our tents, wearied and exhausted from our trek down the mountain. For once I didn't need to roll up a pillow out of my spare clothes—the muskeg was so soft that I simply sank into my tent floor as if it were a bed of pillows. It was wonderfully comfortable, and untroubled as we were by any further thoughts of demon creatures, I soon fell into a deep sleep.

24

RETURN

*The number of apparitions inhabiting the forests and barrens
is rather small considering the opportunity for the play of
fear-inspired imagination offered by these immense solitudes.*
—Frank G. Speck, *Naskapi*, 1935

Z ACH AND I WOKE in the early morning feeling refreshed
after a comfortable night's sleep. Sparrows sang nearby
among the dwarf tamaracks as we took down our tents. It was a
cold morning, and we felt grateful there were no bugs. Muskeg,
we both agreed, made for an excellent night's sleep; we'd found
it luxuriously comfortable, especially after the hard rocks of the
mountains. Best of all, we'd somehow avoided sinking into the
water or getting wet. Inside my tent I'd laid out an emergency
blanket on the floor, and this had kept my sleeping bag nice
and dry.

We continued our trek overland back to the basecamp,
making fine progress until we came back to the thickets and
steep hills. Here we experienced the same difficulties as before,
battling our way through jungles of alders and over mazes of
dead spruces. Our clothing again snagged and tore on the sharp,

snapped-off branches, but we kept up a decent pace all the same, and eventually found our way back to the canoe and our camp.

It appeared exactly as we'd left it—nothing had been disturbed, and even the watertight barrel loaded with our food rations was untouched. I tapped the canoe affectionately; I never did like to leave it behind. We were inseparable friends after all the adventures we'd been through together. The trail camera, too, was still lashed to the balsam fir. If it had recorded anything, we wouldn't know until after our expedition, when we'd be able to take the memory card out of it. It seemed more than likely an animal or two must have wandered by our camp since we'd been gone.

We celebrated our successful return with some dried fruit we'd stashed in the barrel and fresh water from the nearby stream. But there was still plenty of daylight and long miles ahead of us, so after a brief rest, we hauled the canoe down to the water, reloaded it, and set off downriver. Travelling downstream meant much faster progress than on the way up, when we'd had to battle for every inch against the strong current.

The river's numerous rapids, however, had to be navigated with care, laced as they were with jagged rocks and large boulders. Fortunately, we managed to zigzag around such hazards in each of them with only minimal scrapes, and plunge through the big waves without capsizing. One roaring rapid was a bit more technical, so we opted to guide our canoe down the side of it, avoiding the rocks in the centre.

There was plenty of wildlife as we descended the river; we saw half a dozen or more ospreys soaring overhead or perched in huge nests atop black spruces. In one thicket, a hawk owl, which are unusual among owls in being active during the day, swooped majestically out of the woods on the bank and across the river right in front of us. Meanwhile whisky jacks flapped lazily over the water, while Canada geese, pintails, mergansers, and other ducks drifted on the current, not yet having migrated south. In the river, too, were otters, muskrats, and the odd beaver, which slapped its tail at us as we passed.

We spent the night camping on a mud flat behind some driftwood logs. Again we slept soundly, although the hooting of an owl did wake me once. The next morning, too, I heard the strange calls of some sandhill cranes echoing across the marshes. But our spirits were high, feeling as we did that the hardest part of our journey was now well behind us.

When we reached the brackish waters of Lake Melville again, we pressed on along the coast, paddling hard against stiff winds. At one point a storm sprang up on us, creating big waves and a lashing rain that soaked us. But we pressed on through it, paddling over the swells and following the spruce-lined shore. That night we camped in another marsh where all the ground was sodden and decent drinking water difficult to find. We made the best of it, though, and again found that, all things considered, we preferred sleeping on wet ground to solid rock. These marshes were a little eerie, with owls and sandhill cranes calling across them in the night. Those kinds of noises, echoing out of misty marshes, or dreary swamps, or inaccessible mountains, are just the sort of thing that sets the imagination running.

But Zach and I paid them little attention. We'd unravelled the mystery and deconstructed the monster behind it, and our thoughts were now untroubled by any night sounds. I reflected how behind most myths or legends is usually something ordinary, which becomes embellished. People fear the unknown; and it was unknown animals that had sparked the legend. Similarly, on the Labrador coast, as in other sea ports, ancient mariners and sailors had their own legends of things that lurked in the deep; krakens and sea monsters, which were likely inspired by sightings of real but unfamiliar creatures, such as giant squids.

The final bit of our journey entailed paddling across the remainder of Lake Melville, then back through the maze of alder-shrouded islands, and finally up the mighty Churchill River. Battling the huge river's powerful current was made even more difficult by fierce opposing winds, which took every last ounce of our combined strength to make headway against. With painstaking effort we slowly overcame the current and winds, until at last we reached the gravel parking lot on the outskirts of town. We were exhausted but in high spirits after the successful completion of our journey, and more than a little hungry after weeks of bland rations.

Once there, we split up. Zach set off on foot to retrieve his vehicle in town, while I remained on the riverbank with the canoe and the rest of our gear. After a little while an older man came leisurely walking along the bank in my direction. He was perhaps seventy or so, heavyset, with a friendly look.

"You just coming in or just heading out?" he asked.

"Just returned," I replied.

"Ah." He nodded. "Where did you go?"

"Downriver, then east along the coast of Lake Melville, then upriver and eventually into the Mealy Mountains and back again," I said.

"My God," replied the man, "in just that little canoe?"

"Yes sir."

He shook his head. "Good on ya. I wouldn't want to be out there in that. I only canoed three times in my life. First time I tipped. Second time I tipped. Third time I tipped. And then I said: never again! And that was forty years ago and I've never set foot in a canoe since."

I nodded.

"That's a big country out there. Three hundred thousand square kilometres! Wilderness everywhere," the man said enthusiastically.

"Very big," I agreed.

Then the man's expression changed and his voice dropped low. "Did you see anything strange when you were out there?" he asked.

"Well . . . nothing we couldn't ultimately explain. Some odd noises in the night. Sandhill cranes and owls calling."

"Sandhill cranes!"

It turned out he was a keen birder, and we fell to discussing the birds of Labrador at some length. There was a debate, he said, among the birding community, over whether sandhill cranes bred in Labrador at all. There was apparently no solid proof, and given the remoteness and vastness of the mountains and swamps, verifying whether they were there or not was difficult. He was keenly interested that I'd heard them—as he said he'd never seen one in all his many years in Labrador. Their call I knew well, as sandhill cranes migrated over the woods near my home. I'd also seen them regularly breeding in the Hudson Bay Lowlands.

We were still chatting about birds when Zach drove into the parking lot. The man waved and wished me well, and then carried on with his walk while Zach and I loaded the car. When everything was packed and the canoe secured on the roof, we bid farewell to the mountains and drove off down the dusty road.

—

The drive home took another three days, bringing us back across the vast wilderness of Labrador and northern Quebec, then along the St. Lawrence and Lake Ontario, and finally to the rolling fields and pine woods of Norfolk County, my home for the past year. I spent much of the drive deep in thought, brooding over the nature of myths and monsters. Zach meanwhile fulfilled his craving for a hot shower and a breakfast that wasn't granola bars. When we arrived back in my driveway and had the canoe and gear unpacked and put away, we discussed our journey.

"Well I think that satisfied my curiosity," I said.

"Mine too." Zach nodded. "Although it would've been nice to have actually seen a wolverine."

"That'll have to wait for another day," I said.

"Well, if you ever need an expedition partner on short notice again to investigate some historical mystery or explore some wild river or anything else, you can count me in," said Zach.

"Certainly," I replied. Zach had proved to be an excellent wilderness companion. In fact, I decided to gift him a memento from our adventure—the broken canoe paddle, which had snapped in the rapids, and which he'd converted to a walking stick by day, and a vampire stake by night.

"Are you sure you want to part with it? It did go across the Arctic with you," said Zach as I handed him the paddle in two pieces.

"You keep it," I said. "It may come in handy, and I have my other one still."

"Thanks," replied Zach. "Well, I'd better be off. I've got a lot of work to catch up on."

He waved and climbed into his car, then took off down the road.

Feeling satisfied in having unravelled an old mystery and accomplished what we'd set out to do, I unlocked the door to our little home and went inside. My wife, Alexandria, wasn't home, but in anticipation of my return she'd thoughtfully restocked the cupboard with my favourite tea. To celebrate, I put the kettle on. As I waited for it to boil, I returned my backpack to its usual place beside my desk and tossed my explorer hat atop my bookshelf.

Then, with a steaming cup of green tea in hand, I sat down at my desk. Even though I'd just gotten back I found myself already longing again for the deep dark woods with its fresh air and its mysteries. That made me think of the trail camera. I was curious to see what animals it had captured; maybe a porcupine or two, certainly several moose, probably bears, and if we were really lucky, perhaps a wolverine.

But when I popped the HDMI card into my laptop, I found far fewer recordings than I'd anticipated. Glancing at the thumbnails, my confusion deepened—a lot of them looked black, and the others, from what I could tell without clicking on them, were just Zach and I stepping in front of the camera as we set it up and took it down.

The other recordings were inexplicable. When I played them, they were mostly just dark images, with rustling noises in the background. Occasionally interrupting the darkness were flashes of indistinct movement, and once or twice a strange fluttering light right up against the camera lens. In a few recordings something seemed to rumble or shake the camera. There were thirty-six separate recordings like this, one after another, all from the same night—the night we'd camped beside the overgrown ruins of Traverspine. It made me slightly uneasy.

For a moment I wondered whether the camera had malfunctioned. And yet it had clearly been working properly as Zach and I had been recorded just fine whenever we stepped in front of it. But somehow there wasn't a single animal on video from our entire journey, not even a squirrel—almost as if *something* had kept the animals away. Other than ourselves, the only movement that had tripped the camera's sensor had been made by that mysterious indistinct thing with the faint rustling noise.

I examined the time stamp on the videos. The camera had first been tripped at 10:08 p.m. the night we camped at the ruins. That must have been only minutes after Zach and I had gone into our tents—as if something had been quietly watching us by the fire, and had waited until we'd crawled into our tents to emerge from the woods. Over the next fifty-four minutes, between 10:08 p.m. and 11:02 p.m., something had repeatedly set off the camera's motion-activated sensor.

I tried to think of a rational explanation. Maybe it'd been insects, like a mosquito or a blackfly, flying in front of the lens. But it occurred to me that the night at the ruins had been cold, frosty in fact, and therefore too cold for bugs. Maybe it was the wind shaking some branches?

But it was odd the wind had never set off the camera on any other night. And why were the recordings dark? The camera was equipped with an infrared flash, which unlike an ordinary flash, is invisible to the naked eye; this enables the camera to film in the dark by lighting up what it records without letting what's being filmed notice. But for some reason, on these recordings it was too dark to make anything out distinctly. Yet whenever Zach or I had stepped in front of the sensor we were lit up properly.

I went back to my original thought—that the camera must have somehow malfunctioned—but I still couldn't explain how it had also recorded us walking in front of it perfectly fine every night. My bewilderment only increased when I remembered that in the morning at Traverspine I'd found the tracks of what I thought was a moose sunk into the ground only a few feet in front of the lens—*giant pointed tracks like cloven hoofs, with only two big toes*. The tracks had come straight from the dark woods. And yet there was no moose on any of the recordings.

A chill went down my spine and a strange feeling began to form in the pit of my stomach. Irrational thoughts started creeping into my brain. What had Zach and I awakened from that long-abandoned place? Were demon creatures reflectionless? Had it followed us the whole time? I remembered the whispering noises in the night—and all the things in those old accounts we never fully explained: the missing sled dogs, the tapping noise at the doors and windows.

I repressed a shudder, exited the program, and abruptly shut my laptop ... the camera had to have malfunctioned. That was all. There wasn't any other explanation.

With that, I grabbed my walking stick and hat, and headed for the woods ...

AFTERWORD

Wilderness is not a luxury but a necessity of the human spirit, and as
vital to our lives as water and good bread. A civilization which destroys
what little remains of the wild . . . is cutting itself off from its origins . . .
—Edward Abbey, *Desert Solitaire*, 1968

They have this individual gain by living in the wilderness—not by
living in a community. All these individual spiritual beliefs and values
and practices of each individual came from living in the wilderness.
—Omushkego elder Louis Bird, *The Spirit Lives in the Mind*, 2007

WHAT HAPPENS WHEN there are no more deep dark
woods? No more remote, inaccessible mountains? What
happens to so much of our culture, folklore, and shared human
heritage when we've cleared the last ancient forest or so hacked
it up with trails, signs, parking lots, wifi hotspots, and visitor
centres that it barely retains any resemblance to the wild thing
it once was? What happens when solitude becomes impossible
to find in an ever more crowded world? What happens when
we've dynamited and mined the last wild mountains, leaving

only a sad remnant intersected with highways and resorts? To be sure, not all these things are bad all the time—I just think there's something special, magical even, about Earth's truly wild places.

The world's once mighty forests and wild mountains, pristine lakes and other natural spaces, have always been a fount of inspiration for much of human imagination and creativity. Even if most people seldom or never set foot in any of these places, historically the mere fact of their existence on the edges of our cities and settled areas has profoundly shaped the way humans made sense of our world—as a place brimming with mysteries and half-whispered possibilities. Sure, some of that took the form of monsters, trolls, spirits, elves, or other beings lurking in the unknown wilderness, but that's part of what makes our world such a fascinating place. When we lose wilderness, we lose more than just natural habitats that provide us with clean air, fresh water, and a place for wildlife to roam. We lose something intangible—something that runs deep in our collective psyches and heritage—the canvas on which so much of human culture has been painted.

I'm not suggesting we ought to go back to living in caves and getting eaten by monsters of the wild. That'd be foolish and probably unlikely to attract a lot of popular support. I do think, however, that we ought to at least have such places left on Earth for wildlife to roam free, and for the human spirit to do likewise. Some will probably argue that outer space could fill this cultural void (although it wouldn't do much to help the animals). But outer space will never be accessible to the vast majority; for most of us, we can only ever experience firsthand that feeling of awe, mystery, grandeur, and wonder from the beauty and sublimity of the natural world.

Yet scientists continue to warn that wilderness is disappearing at an alarming rate worldwide, and along with it much of Earth's biodiversity. But even now it's not too late to turn back the clock; it still lies within our grasp to find the will to preserve vast wild places, and even to go beyond that by restoring natural landscapes that were previously lost. For example, with a few easy steps we could reduce light pollution in our countryside and around our cities, restoring something as simple yet soul-inspiring as the ability to see the stars. We can also build land bridges or wildlife overpasses across busy highways, connecting pockets of forests in more populated areas and allowing animals to roam more freely. Indeed, the positive effects of having wild nature on our doorsteps are profound and well-attested: it can offer a release from the stress of modern life, as well as reawaken our connection to nature and our sense of mystery and awe at the natural world. More than that, preserving vast wild places ensures that there will always be metaphorical blank spaces on our maps, dark woods and vast mountains, hunting grounds for our imaginations to soar—to think and dream that anything may be possible, and to remember where we came from. That, in my estimation, is well worth saving.

ACKNOWLEDGMENTS

WITHOUT THE ASSISTANCE of numerous individuals, this book wouldn't have happened. I've been very fortunate to benefit from the expertise and support of an excellent team at Penguin Random House Canada. First and foremost, I'm once again indebted to Nick Garrison, my editor. Nick's early and enthusiastic encouragement of the idea for this book helped make it a reality. For that I'm grateful, as few writers can be as lucky as I am to find such an editor. Nick's insights and suggestions on the manuscript sharpened the focus and expanded the content. I must also thank Nicole Winstanley, Penguin Canada's publisher, for her continued belief in the value of my stories. Without her, they might never have appeared in print. Alanna McMullen, as editorial assistant, played numerous behind-the-scenes roles in getting this book ready for publication, and for that I'm most grateful.

Karen Alliston, the copy editor, carefully scrutinized the manuscript with a keen eye and helped correct any mistakes, as did proofreader Catherine Dorton. Both of their contributions are much appreciated. Any errors that may remain are mine alone. On the publicity side of things, Beth Cockeram, Penguin Canada's marketing manager, and Sharon Gill, the book's publicist, helped to get the word out as well as organize book events. I'm grateful to both of them for their hard work. Bonnie Maitland, as sales director, has also helped the book find an audience. Penguin's managing editor, David Ross, kept everything running smoothly and on schedule (never an easy task with an author who is frequently out of contact in the wild). The talented Emma Dolan designed the book's cover. I thank all of them for their excellent work. My literary agent, Rick Broadhead, has been everything an author could want in an agent, and for his tireless work, I'm grateful.

On the expedition side of things, I must thank the Royal Canadian Geographical Society for their ongoing support of my work. In particular, I thank John Geiger for his steadfast encouragement. I'm also indebted to Alvaro Geiger, for providing some crucial help in securing research materials for me. I especially want to thank Peter and Brigitte Westaway for their incredible support. I was fortunate to cross paths with Peter and Brigitte a few years ago and they have since been instrumental in making my expeditions happen. Indeed, I'm thrilled to now hold the position of Westaway Explorer-in-Residence at the Royal Canadian Geographical Society, named in their honour. Their support and belief in my expeditions have made it possible for me to pursue many exploration ideas that otherwise would have remained purely hypothetical. For that, I'm very grateful. I must also thank my last-minute expedition partner, Zach Junkin, who was an excellent adventure companion. He was also kind enough to share his diary of our expedition with me, which helped make this book as detailed as possible.

The staff at *Them Days* magazine, a Labrador journal devoted to local history, were also very helpful in answering my questions.

I was also fortunate to have family and friends read the book before publication and offer valuable feedback. I thank Mark Shoalts, Catherine Shoalts, Ben Shoalts, and Ocean Shoalts for their help and suggestions. Graham Smith and Paxton Allewell, in particular, were also very keen-eyed readers with many thoughtful comments. I'm indebted to both of them.

I must also thank my teachers, who encouraged my love of literature and legends. Looking back at my public school education, I consider myself lucky that I had teachers and a curriculum that nurtured a love of reading, the outdoors, and history. My time at McMaster University earning a doctorate in history, although not directly related to the contents of this book, helped me conduct the research for it. I'm lucky to have benefited from an excellent program at that university, with an outstanding trio of supervisors who sharpened my thinking and made me a much better historian than I'd otherwise be. For that, I'm indebted to Dr. Ken Cruikshank, Dr. John Weaver, and Dr. Megan Armstrong.

Above all, I must thank Alexandria (Aleksia) for her easy-going encouragement of my expeditions (indeed, she sometimes suggests I remain in the wilderness longer), her invaluable insights as an editor and sounding board for ideas, and much else besides. For her, and her assistance, I'm very lucky and grateful.

ADAM SHOALTS is a historian, archaeologist, geographer, and Westaway Explorer-in-Residence at the Royal Canadian Geographical Society. Shoalts holds a PhD from McMaster University where his research examined the influence Indigenous oral traditions had on fur traders in the subarctic and Pacific Northwest. He is also the author of *Alone Against the North*, *A History of Canada in Ten Maps*, and *Beyond the Trees*, all of them national bestsellers. He enjoys long walks in the woods. Follow his adventures on Facebook and Instagram.